D1082184

Formula
for
Happiness

Formula for Happiness

by Spiros Zodhiates, Th.D.

An exegetical exposition of
I Corinthians 4:6—21
from the Greek Text.

The first five verses of I Corinthians 4 are covered in a
196 page volume entitled *You and Public Opinion*,
published by AMG Publishers,
Chattanooga, TN 37421.

AMG PUBLISHERS
CHATTANOOGA, TN 37421

COVER DESIGN FLORENCE ANDERSON
COPYRIGHT 1980 BY SPIROS ZODHIATES
PRINTED IN THE UNITED STATES OF AMERICA

ISBN 0-89957-046-1

Dedicated to
S. JOHN DAVID
who in my estimation is a perfect example of
a sacrificing disciple of Jesus Christ for and
among his suffering fellow people of
India.

PREFACE

Look at your fingers. They are different, and yet they are similar. But being part of the same hand they co-exist and cooperate with each other in order to accomplish the hand's purpose.

The same God who made different and unequal fingers on your hand also made human beings to differ from each other. Our differences are not so much due to the cruelty of society, of environment, and circumstances, as they are to the fact that such differences were actually planned and executed by God, the Creator.

Consider I Corinthians 4:7: "For who maketh thee to differ from another? and what hast thou that thou didst not receive?" God is responsible for our differences, but not for our quarrels. We are different for the purpose of complementing each other, and not for the purpose of fighting each other in the struggle for "the survival of the fittest."

Besides our created differences, there are also differences which exist because of our own personal choices. We *choose* to be different, to act differently, and we choose different life styles. Not all poor people, for instance, are poor because they have to be. Some are poor because they choose to be, in order that through their sacrifice they may better serve God and help others. By making such a choice, do such people thereby deprive themselves of the highest possible joy in life? Who is the happiest in this life; he who has much, and has achieved success, prominence and fame, or he who through self-abnegation is of most benefit to God and humanity?

These are the questions Paul discussed as he wrote to the proud, quarreling Christians at Corinth. He contrasted their selfishness and his sacrifice as an apostle. Who proved to be better off, ultimately?

These are really hot questions which every thinking Christian must ask:

How much material goods and riches should I accumulate for my own benefit, and how much fame should I seek? How much of my time and possessions should I place at God's disposal? Is there more joy in sacrifice or abundance?

Should I only have fellowship with those who fully agree with me? How did Paul treat Apollos, with whom he disagreed? When is accommodation a compromise? When should we disregard the criticism of other Christians? Is it compromise to reshape some of our own views that may not be fundamental? Who is to tell what aspect of truth is so fundamental that it cannot be held variantly by Christians? Before you call anybody a compromiser, or accept that accusation against yourself by others, you ought to read Paul's thesis in I Corinthians 4:6-21. It has searched my own life as few other portions of Scripture have ever done. I hope it will challenge you, also.

Blessed meditation!

Spiros Zodhiates

CONTENTS

How Much Can We Alter Our Views and Conduct without Compromising?

"And these things, brethren, I have in a figure transferred to myself and to Apollos for your sakes; that ye might learn in us not to think of men above that which is written, that no one of you be puffed up for one against another" (I Cor. 4:6).

A Difficult Passage of Scripture

First Corinthians 4:6 is one of the most difficult verses in the New Testament, especially the first part. In my 20,000-volume library I found only two sermons on this verse. One was by Llynfi Davies, preached at Canaan Congregational Church in Swansea, Wales, in 1930 (recorded in the *Christian World Pulpit*, vol. 118, pp. 22-3). The other was by I. M. Haldeman, who preached it in 1910 at the First Baptist Church of New York City, of which he was pastor for 51 years. The first sermon deals with the first part of the verse, and the second sermon deals with the last part of the verse. Much of what I shall expound will be expressive of the thoughts of these two preachers, who dared to tackle this unusual verse.

To make the meaning of this verse clear, we

11

must first recall what preceded it. You remember that Paul was criticized by the Corinthian Christians as an unfaithful servant and steward of the mysteries of God. He defended himself (see I Corinthians 4:3, 5) by saying that it mattered very little to him what others thought of him, whether it was the Corinthians, or any other man, or even what he thought of himself. He wasn't seeking the praise of the Corinthians, but the praise of God.

He then goes on to give them some straight-forward advice that may seem like scolding. He closes this 4th chapter with the words, "What will ye? shall I come unto you with a rod, or in love, and in the spirit of meekness?" They sought to criticize him. He now tries to instruct them. He considers such instruction to be part of his apostolic mission if he is to be faithful, as he said every minister of Christ ought to be. The words "these things" in verse 6 must therefore be taken to mean the instructions that are to follow. And as usual, when he is about to reprimand them, he calls them "brethren," to assure them that he is doing it in love.

But he tells them something else, which is very difficult to interpret without a basic understanding of the Greek word Paul used. It is *metescheematisa* (*metascheematizoo*), which in the Authorized Version is rendered "I have in a figure transferred to myself," and in the New International Version, "I have applied these things to myself."

Metascheematizoo is made up of the preposition *meta,* meaning "after," implying a change from the present, and the verb *scheematizoo,* meaning "to assume a certain form, shape, figure, posture, or position." There is no doubt that the verb here is used transitively, transferring the action to Paul himself and to Apollos. It is as if he were saying, "I placed a different shape upon myself and Apollos."

The tense is the first aorist, indicative mood, active voice, which means that this is something he decided to do once and for all. It was a philosophy of life that he adopted in dealing with the Corinthians.

Before we proceed to examine the specific meaning of Paul's word in this context, it is necessary for us to determine the true meaning of *metascheematizoo* and the substantive from which it is derived, *scheema,* as contrasted to another verb, *metamorphoomai* or *metamorphoo-omai,* commonly translated "transfigure," which is derived from the substantive *morphee,* "figure." The distinction between these two words—*scheema,* from which we get our English word "schematic," and *morphee,* from which the English word "metamorphosis" is derived—is very important.

The word *scheema* is found in I Corinthians 7:31 and Philippians 2:8. In both instances it is correctly translated "fashion." "For the fashion of this world [*kosmou,* 'material universe'] passeth away." The image here is probably drawn from the shifting scenes of a theater. But the cosmos itself, the material universe, abides. In the New Testament we never read of "the end of the world," *telos tou kosmou,* that is, the material universe, but only of the age, *aeon* or *aeons* (*aioon* or *aioonos*). Thus the shape of the material universe changes, but not the universe itself.

The second use of the word *scheema,* in Philippians 2:8, has serious theological implications, as distinguished from the word *morphee,* which occurs in Philippians 2:6, 7 and Mark 16:12. To bring out the distinction between the derivative compound verbs *metascheematizoo* and *metamorphoo-omai,* it is necessary to examine the distinction between the two nouns *scheema* and *morphee,* especially in the Christological passage in Philippians 2:6-8. We will

13

take this up in detail further on in this study.

"Refashioning": The Process by Which God Became Man

In this section we shall begin our examination of a number of Greek words that are essential to the understanding of I Corinthians 4:6.

In Philippians 2:6-8, speaking of the Lord Jesus Christ in His eternal state and His incarnation, Paul writes:

"Who [the eternal *Logos,* Christ], being in the form [*morphee*] of God, thought it not robbery to be equal with God:

"But made himself of no reputation [in the Greek, emptied himself], and took upon him the form [*morpheen*] of a servant, and was made in the likeness of men:

"And being found in fashion [*scheemati,* the dative singular of *scheema*] as a man, he humbled himself, and became obedient unto death, even the death of the cross."

Paul is telling us two important things here about the Lord Jesus Christ: 1) That in His eternal state He was in the form of God (*en morphee Theou*); and 2) that in His incarnation He assumed the form of a servant (*morpheen doulou laboon*).

The word *morphee* here is not explicitly *ousia,* "substance," or *phusis,* "nature," as Church Fathers like Ambrose (Ep. 46), and Gregory of Nyssa (Con. Eunom. 4) used it against the Arians who rejected the deity of Christ. But implicitly it does refer to the divine nature of our Lord. No one could be in the form (*morphee*) of God who was not God. *Morphee* signifies the form as it is, the utterance of the inner life. Therefore it means "mode of existence." Only God could have the mode of existence of God. But the One who had

14

been thus from eternity *en morphee,* in the form of God, as He Himself told us in John 17:5, took at His incarnation *morpheen doulou,* the form of a servant. The actuality of His incarnation is herein implied. It was not a mere appearance of humanity, as it was not an appearance of deity. It was true deity before His incarnation, and true humanity at His incarnation. There was nothing imaginary about it.

But His manner of existence in His incarnation was that of *doulos,* "servant," a bondman, a slave. The Greek word *doulos* refers to one who is in a permanent relation of servitude to another, his will swallowed up in the will of the other. Certainly this was not Christ's relationship toward man. That is why He is never referred to as a *doulos anthroopoon,* "a servant or slave of men." He became identified with the human race in the capacity of *diakonos anthroopoon* (see John 13:4, 5, and Matt. 20:28), a servant of men in that this indicated His activity on behalf of the work He came to do. He did not subject His will to man; He worked on behalf of man.

Here in Philippians 2:7 we are told Christ became a servant, slave, *doulos,* not of man but of God. Being equal with God, being in the form, *morphee,* of God, He emptied Himself of the glory of that form and took upon Himself the form of a servant or slave, *doulos,* of God. The mode of His personal existence changed from that of God to that of a servant, a slave. As God He ruled; as God-man He ministered. That was humiliation.

The next clause we consider is in Philippians 2:8, which says, "And being found in fashion [*scheemati*] as a man." The word is different here. *Scheema* here signifies Christ's whole outward presentation, His bodily form as a man.

First, we have His eternal deity.

Second, we have His true humanity, what He

15

became in addition to what He was. The *Logos* permanently took upon Himself true humanity.

Third, we have His shape perceived by men: "And being found [*heuretheis*] by men as man." In no way did Jesus appear to humans as any different from the other children of men. By the Father, He was recognized as being equal with Himself. By men He was recognized as being of the same fashion or shape as themselves.

When we come to the two verbs *metascheematizoo* and *metamorpho-oo*, we find the distinction made even clearer. "If I were to change a Dutch garden into an Italian," says Trench, "this would be *metascheematismos*, refashioning. This would still be a garden but of a different style. But if I were to transform a garden into something wholly different, as into a city, this would be *metamorphoosis*. For instance Satan is said to *metascheematizesthai*—to take the shape of, or disguise himself as, an angel of light (II Cor. 11:14). He can take the whole outward semblance of such. But to any such change of his it would be impossible to apply the *metamorphousthai*, taking a different form: for this would imply a change not external but internal, not of appearances but of essence, which lies quite beyond his power.

"The two verbs are used in Romans 12:2, 'And be not conformed—*suscheematizesthe*—become the same in fashion, outward appearance—to this world (*aeon*—age): but be ye transformed—*metamorphousthe*—changed in form, essence—by the renewing of your mind. . . .' This is an abiding deep change in you as the Spirit of God alone can work in you (II Cor. 3:18)."

(See R. C. Trench, *Synonyms of the New Testament*, pp. 263-4.)

16

When a Dispute Arises Between Christians

We conclude from our examination of the verb *metescheematisa* so far that it does not mean what the Authorized Version translates it as: "I have in a figure transferred to myself." This would infer that Paul was blaming himself and Apollos for the inconsistencies and divisions among the Corinthians. It would be as if he were saying, "None of you are to blame; I myself and Apollos are the culprits." But though Paul was a humble man, he never assumed a false humility. He was far too honest for that. He did not try to excuse the guilty but to correct them. And the only way he could correct was to place the blame where it belonged.

The verb *metescheematisa* means "to refashion." It is used by Paul alone in the New Testament, and on only three occasions: in our text, in II Corinthians 11:13-15, and Philippians 3:21. In the latter two instances it is used with reference to Satan fashioning himself into, or disguising himself as, an angel of light, and in the Philippians reference with regard to the fact that Christ would change our body till it resembled the body of His glory.

Why should Paul mention Apollos along with himself in this context of I Corinthians 4:6? It doesn't seem to make sense. We know, however, that there were differences between himself and Apollos, even as the Corinthians had differences among themselves. He is trying to correct the Corinthian divisions. But how about the division between himself and Apollos? He has rejected the Corinthian criticism about unfaithfulness, but he confesses that he is willing to refashion his relationship with Apollos, even as he is pleading with the Corinthians to do among themselves.

"I am willing to do what I am asking you to do," he says in effect. He had just said that he did not judge himself; nevertheless he is ready to change certain outward appearances for the sake of the Corinthians. It was not actually his character that was involved, which would have been the case if the verb *metamorpho-oo* had been used. *Morphee,* as we saw earlier, refers to the inner self, and *scheema* to the outward. His standing up against Apollos may in itself have been right and necessary, but his dispute with Apollos apparently was not a good example for the constantly disputing Corinthians.

We, too, must be willing to avoid even the appearance of evil, even if what we are doing may not be evil at all. A dispute with a brother may be fully justified in itself, but if it harms others it may be wise to change our ways. Truth is essential, but how we apply it in an ever-changing world should be subject to our constant scrutiny.

Refashioning our conduct need not involve change of or compromise with the truth. Paul was merely adapting the truth to the case in point, with a view to saving a church so dear to him as the one at Corinth, to which he had devoted eighteen months of his missionary labors. He felt that none of his own interpersonal relationships should be allowed to harm the Church.

How wise we would be to follow Paul's gracious example. Let's ask ourselves the question: What will my public dispute with another do to a local church or to the cause of Christ anywhere and everywhere?'' And then let's be ready to refashion our conduct for the sake of the Church of Christ and our testimony before the world.

Now what were the matters in question between Paul and Apollos? You remember that they had both ministered to the church at Corinth. Paul had left there at the end of his second missionary journey and had proceeded to Jerusalem. Before

Paul had returned to Ephesus, Apollos—after about three months' training in Gospel truths in that city by Aquila and Priscilla—had proceeded to Corinth. We know nothing of the exact nature of his ministry there apart from a brief summary in the Acts: "He mightily convinced the Jews, and that publicly, shewing by the scriptures that Jesus was Christ" (Acts 18:28). But we know that by the time Paul had returned to Ephesus on his third journey Apollos had also reached that city with his ministry at Corinth over. We know further that he had barely reached Ephesus before Paul received news that the church at Corinth was being rocked by factions.

Now, in the face of these facts, we may wonder whether the nature of Apollos' ministry at Corinth had had something to do with the deplorable condition of the church. He was faithfully proclaiming sound doctrine, preaching that "Jesus was Christ." He may not have consciously contributed to the raising of the parties causing strife and divisions in the church. But it is possible that his method of presenting the Gospel had been such as to cultivate the ground in which obnoxious weeds might grow. As a young and inexperienced minister, full of enthusiasm and good intentions, but following a veteran in the ministry such as Paul, he may have inadvertently blundered in some way, and then wondered why things were unaccountably, to him, going wrong. What some of these problems may have been we shall consider next.

Did Paul Write the Epistle to the Hebrews, and Why?

In order to understand a man, we must know something of his background and how it affects his character. Thus, in seeking to understand the matters at issue between Paul and Apollos, we must ask ourselves just who this man Apollos was.

Scripture tells us that he was an Alexandrian, and accordingly of a philosophical trend of mind (Acts 18:24). We may be justified in assuming that his Alexandrian training and his necessarily imperfect knowledge of the Gospel as preached by his predecessor Paul, in the church at Corinth, caused his ministry there to whet the philosophical appetites of the Corinthians. The desire for speculation, once awakened, caused the ground to be unintentionally prepared for conflicting opinions regarding the Scriptures and Christ.

Did Apollos' Alexandrian training get the better of him in his preaching? Did he, an Alexandrian Jew, suggest a different view of the Law from Paul's view? How did he "mightily convince the Jews" at Corinth (Acts 18:28)? Was it by presenting them with a more acceptable view of the Law and Christ's relation to it, such as we find in Hebrews, than Paul's usual view of the Law as an intolerable yoke?

Why does Paul, in this very epistle to the Corinthians, before dealing with the question of factions, state that when he was in Corinth he had determined not to know anything among them except Jesus Christ, and Him crucified (I Cor. 2:2)? Is there a suggestion that someone had followed him at Corinth who had preached Christ in a different way? Is there also a suggestion that he himself could have preached the Gospel in a philosophical way had he been so minded?

Surely Paul's theology does not exclude such a possibility in certain circumstances. In all this, was Paul quietly alluding to the nature of Apollos' ministry in the Corinthian church? And did he have Apollos in mind, though not naming him, when he followed with his disapproval of the wisdom of the world in the same chapter (I Cor. 2:4)? Is not

Apollos' ministry somewhere in the background of Paul's mind as he writes the second chapter of I Corinthians, which leads directly to the question of parties?

Questions like these cannot help coming to one's mind in the light of the fresh statement that Paul had refashioned some matters that concerned himself and Apollos. That Apollos was not happy over what had happened at Corinth is manifest from the fact that he declined to return to Corinth at Paul's suggestion (I Cor. 16:12). Possibly he was reluctant to carry back the refashioned matter for the church's consideration.

Llynfi Davies believes that the refashioned work is the Epistle to the Hebrews; that Paul deliberately cast that epistle into an Alexandrian mold in order to save the church at Corinth. Scholars have hesitated to label the Epistle to the Hebrews Pauline in the accepted sense of the word. And yet there is much in it that is Pauline. But it does differ from the Pauline conception of the Law, and of faith especially, though not in its thought of the pre-eminence of Christ. But there is no reason Paul could not have written it if he had made up his mind to "refashion" his message in view of the circumstances.

I believe that in the Epistle to the Hebrews we have in an Alexandrian mold the things refashioned between Paul and Apollos, the Alexandrian Jew. I think it logical to assume that things had gone unintentionally wrong with Apollos' ministry at Corinth. He had preached a view of the Scriptures and of Christ that was not in keeping with Paul's Gospel of Christ crucified. So powerful was the party associated with Apollos' name that it dominated the church and threatened its peace and unity.

Comparing notes, so to speak, with Apollos at

Ephesus, Paul embodied the results in a work that would indicate to the church how far they could safely proceed on the lines suggested by Apollos' preaching. That work is the epistle known as Hebrews. Study it with this in mind. That was Paul's method of refashioning. He practiced it also in what he wrote to the Corinthians concerning their speaking in tongues, a practice quite divergent from the historical instances. In those we have Jews (Acts 2), Gentiles (Acts 10), and the disciples of John (Acts 19), enabled by the Holy Spirit to speak instantly and temporarily in languages unknown to them but understood by those who heard them. This element of immediate comprehension was missing from the Corinthian practice, which was speaking in an incomprehensible so-called unknown tongue.

Paul refashions these things in saying to the Corinthians that the point of tolerance is if things are done decently and in order, not giving an impression to others that the one thus speaking is a maniac; and that others understand what is being said through an interpreter. Paul is a master at refashioning certain matters that do not affect the faith once delivered to the saints. In all this there was no compromise with truth; only a way of presenting truth in a way suited to the comprehension of those to whom he was addressing himself.

The Humility That Indicates True Greatness

In ascribing the authorship of the Epistle to the Hebrews to Paul, we have seen that it was written as a refashioning of the truth to meet a specific need. Therefore we are not to look for his usual doctrinal thoughts. It expresses, not his own customary way of thinking, but his considered examination of Apollos' way of thinking. Again we stress, this is not compromise but refashioning. It was the veteran minister's way of getting his younger colleague out of a very unpleasant situation.

It follows from this that the usual considerations advanced against the Pauline origin of the epistle become ineffective, for we are not now called upon to account for the differences between this work and the usual work of Paul. It is definitely not a Pauline work in the usual sense of that word, but a Pauline work in the sense that it is Paul's considered examination of Apollos' general point of view, which the Apostle considered safe for the church at Corinth to follow.

The humility of this Apostle is shown in the fact that he was great enough to talk matters over with Apollos at Ephesus, and then, as a consequence, write an epistle that, on the surface, appeared like yielding up the laurel to his rival! How many of us would have the grace to do something similar? That's characteristic of the humility of greatness. What a lesson for our times, when factionalism pervades the Church! How we quibble about differences, ignoring the distressing fact that the Christian Church is divided into so many camps, each one proudly displaying its distinctive label like the Corinthians of old. We readily condemn the factionalism at Corinth, but we have perpetuated their underlying fault in our eagerness to stress our own particular views and practices.

Have we ever thought of the effect our factionalism has upon the world we are all so eager to reach with the Gospel? Let's emulate Paul in putting first things first—the honor and glory of Christ, the souls of men, the welfare of the Church as a whole—and do this by refashioning, if necessary, in such a way as not to alter the fundamental truths of the Gospel, but to meet the needs of others.

The term *di humas,* "for your sakes," is very

23

important. Commentator Lenski is somewhat inconsistent when he translates this expression in I Corinthians 4:6 as "for your sakes" in the text, but in his commentary as "on account of you." This results from his endeavor to justify the traditional view of this verse, which holds that Paul and Apollos were free from the criticism that Paul was leveling at the Corinthians. Paul did not write about himself and Apollos "on account of" the Corinthians, but "for their sakes." He refashioned his position with Apollos to be a good example to the schismatic Corinthians. (It is to be noted, however, that *di humas* with an accusative may mean either "for your sakes" or "on account of you," but one of these two meanings must apply in this particular instance.)

The International Critical Commentary is more accurate when it gives the following paraphrases: "I have transferred these warnings to myself and Apollos *for the purpose* of a covert allusion, *and that for* your sakes, that in our persons you may get instruction." It is as if Paul were saying, "I want you to do not only what we say but what we ourselves do, as fellow-ministers of the Gospel." Would to God that Christian ministers everywhere could turn to their people and say the same. What preachers proclaim in the pulpit, let them exemplify in their daily life and walk with Christ.

What follows in this verse is a telic clause introduced by the conjunction *hina,* "so that, for the purpose of"—so that in us you may learn. "Use us as examples" is the meaning here. That's exactly what Paul says later on in verse 16: "I beseech you, be ye followers of me," that is, become my imitators. That's quite an injunction from a mere man to a whole church. Without the meaning of refashioning in the verb *metescheematisa* in verse 1, it would

24

be difficult to justify such a command. "Imitate me" is quite a thing to say, but Paul could say it because of what he did in his relationship to Apollos.

Observe that he doesn't include Apollos as an additional object for their imitation. Why? Because most of the refashioning was on his part, in spite of the fact that Apollos was the weaker of the two in his knowledge of God's revelation. After all, Paul defends his apostleship (I Cor. 9:1), but he doesn't claim apostleship for Apollos. The refashioning of the greater for the sake of the lesser entitles him to become the object of imitation by others.

Sometimes when people come to us for advice, we know the correct course for them to follow, though we ourselves don't always abide by it. Somewhat humorously we may advise them, "Don't do as I do; do as I say." When this concerns a small matter like following a cooking recipe to the letter, the results may not be catastrophic. But when a Christian minister or teacher, or even a Christ-professing layman, is asked for advice on the Christian life, he had better be pretty sure he practices what he preaches, if he doesn't want to disillusion those who look to him as an example.

Handling the Scriptures Carefully

An inherent danger in seeking to understand and interpret the Scriptures is to read into them more than God intended them to convey. This is not merely the danger of the unlearned, but also of those who have become so familiar with the Scriptures that they begin to take liberties with them, bending them to fit their own particular viewpoints or pet theories of interpretation.

The Apostle Paul was particularly desirous of nipping any such tendency in the bud in the Corinthian church. The occasion of his concern was the matter of the relationship between him and Apollos, which had been misunderstood by the Corinthians. The particular lesson he wanted them to learn as stated in the Authorized Version was "not to think of men above that which is written." But in the Greek, there is no verb; to say that the verb is "to think" is a conjecture. Since the maxim here is given in an elliptical form, without a verb, the insertion of a verb is at best arbitrary. It is equally arbitrary to translate the relative pronoun *ha* primarily as "men." If Paul had thus meant "men," he should have used the relative pronoun in its masculine plural form *hoi*. In this case, the translation in the Authorized Version is incorrect. The relative pronoun *ha* is in the neuter plural, which agrees with the demonstrative pronoun *tauta* (neuter plural of *houtos*) in the first part of this verse, which refers to things, not persons.

The literal translation of this maxim that Paul proposes as basic and fundamental truth is "not more than or beyond what has been written." No one should go beyond what has been written when it comes to the revelation given by God. This is a slap in the face to speculative philosophical thought—a tendency to which the Corinthians were especially prone.

"So that in us ye may learn." Here the verb "learn" in the Greek text is *matheete,* which is in the aorist tense. The word means to cause to know, with a moral bearing to it. (See H. Cremer's *Biblico-Theological Lexicon of the New Testament Greek,* p. 410.) It is as if Paul were saying to the Corinthians that what he is about to tell them to learn and practice is most important; it is basic.

The Greek word *gegraptai* is in the passive voice, which refers to what has been written, and which exists in written form. Paul was, of course, referring to the Old Testament Scriptures, to which he had already alluded in I Corinthians 1:19, 31; and 3:19, 20. To go beyond God's revelation, and add to it one's own elements, or to speculate about things not revealed, is a grave danger, leading to all sorts of fallacies.

This was obviously what was happening in Old Testament times with the false prophets, and it is happening today. What Paul is saying categorically here is that additions to the Scriptures are forbidden when made by unauthorized persons. The outward appearance or *scheema* of truth, the dress, so to speak, the way it is presented, especially in preaching, is flexible, but not the substance, *morphee,* itself. Paul had refashioned his thoughts, as he dealt with Apollos, for the sake of the Corinthians, in the interest of preserving unity among them. But he didn't do this at the price of sacrificing essential written truth.

Read Jeremiah 23:16-32 for its relevance in this connection. "Hearken not unto the words of the prophets that prophesy unto you: they make you vain: they speak a vision of their own heart, and not out of the mouth of the Lord. . . . I have not sent these prophets [saith the Lord], yet they ran: I have not spoken to them, yet they prophesied. . . . I have heard what the prophets said, that prophesy lies in my name, saying, I have dreamed, I have dreamed. How long shall this be in the heart of the prophets that prophesy lies? yea, they are prophets of the deceit of their own heart. . . . I am against the prophets, said the Lord, that steal my words every one from his neighbour . . . that use their tongues, and say, He saith. Behold, I am against them that prophesy false dreams, saith the Lord, and do tell them, and cause my people to err by their lies, and by their lightness; yet I sent them not, nor commanded them: therefore they shall not profit this people at all, saith the Lord."

What Paul is saying in I Corinthians 4:6 is that we must be careful to reject as false any religion or teaching that goes beyond what is written in the Word of God. Man's experiences, dreams, utterances in no matter what tongue, have no validity if they go beyond or against the Scriptures. That is axiomatic and admits of no exceptions. If anyone says that the Scriptures are not sufficient in themselves and need a supplement, we are to reject him. He can only lead us astray. Any religion that puts Scripture in any way in a secondary place, or on a par with other writings or sayings, and demands that it be interpreted according to a particular individual's ideas, is false and not worthy of our consideration.

The books of men have their day and grow obsolete. God's Word is like Himself, "the same yesterday, and to day, and for ever" (Heb. 13:8).

"It Is Written"

The Christian has no quarrel with scholarship, science, or interpretations as such, when it comes to understanding the Bible. They have their place, but they are never to supplant the Scriptures.

Observe that it is not an ignoramus who advised the Corinthian church not to go beyond anything that has been written. If ever a man could have spoken in the words of human wisdom, and with scientific accent, it was the Apostle Paul. He was a member of the Jewish Sanhedrin. He had sat at the feet of Gamaliel, the greatest teacher of his times. He was not only versed in the Hebrew Scriptures, he was thoroughly conversant with Hebrew literature and the Talmud. He knew Latin as well as Hebrew and Greek. When he said that he spoke in tongues more than all the Corinthians, he did not mean the unintelligible ecstatic utterances of the Corinthian church but real languages. He knew Roman philosophy, although it was taught by Greek professors. In fact, Paul had the highest possible education, and a mind second to none. He could analyze and synthesize. He was a logician whose conclusions were reached from premises stated with unfaltering precision.

But Paul didn't speak with the aim of making people admire him, but for the purpose of causing them to be transformed by the power of the cross. He knew the only wisdom worth having was God's, not his. He warned the Colossians against those preachers who would seek to spoil them with philosophy and vain deceit, after the tradition of men (see Col. 2:8). He exhorted Timothy not to be seduced by the "oppositions of science falsely so called" (I Tim. 6:20).

To Paul, the science of that day, the *gnoosis,* "knowledge," of that hour, which laughed at the idea of miracles, tied God up in His own creation, and made Him the slave of the laws and forces that He Himself had created, was neither scientific nor knowledgeable. Such science turns the world into a vast chemical laboratory without a chemist, or a huge engine room with no suspicion of a supreme engineer behind it.

The science that denies the God of the Bible, robs the world of the Christ of the Bible, and finally—shredding the Bible apart page by page— discounts it and wrenches it loose from the pulpit as no longer the inerrant Word of God—that science to Paul was, and would be, contemptible.

The word used for "puffed up" in Greek is *phusiousthe.* It is a Pauline word found only in I Corinthians 4:6, 18, 19; 5:2; 8:1; 13:4, and Colossians

29

2:18. It is derived from *phusi-o-oo,* "to blow up, to puff up." It means figuratively to be proud or arrogant, or, in the passive voice, to become puffed up or conceited.

What Paul is telling the Corinthians here is that he who adds to the Scriptures is likely to be a proud and arrogant person, who looks down upon others because they lack his abilities. He is in the same class as the little girl who went to her priest and confessed her sin of vanity. "What makes you think that?" asked the priest. "Because every morning, when I look into the mirror," she replied, "I think how beautiful I am." "Never fear," said the priest, "that isn't sin; that's just a mistake." How true it is that those who are the proudest in their assumption of the right to think and act above what is written are the most mistaken. They need to humbly accept what God says of them in His Word.

However, the refashioning that Paul did in his relationship to Apollos was not of this nature. It had a double purpose. The first was that the Corinthians might learn that nothing should be placed above the Scriptures. He wanted them to know that the agreement he and Apollos had reached as ministers of the mysteries of God could not stand over against those things already written in the Divine Revelation.

No apostle was to build anything that would overshadow what God had already revealed, and they did not. The New Testament stands on the Old; it cannot stand alone. Note how our Lord stressed that He was the fulfillment of God's promises through the prophets. The expression, "It is written," was continually on His lips. Nothing that any of us might add can supersede that which has already been written.

The second goal that springs from giving the written Word preeminence is that sectarian divisions may be avoided. "That no one of you be puffed up for one against another." The word translated "another" in Greek is *heteron,* meaning "another of a different kind." If anyone adds to God's written revelation, he feels superior because he has something more than another who has not added anything. Setting forth one's own tradition over the Scriptures tends to puff one up with the idea that his religion, his denomination or church, is superior and exclusive.

How true this is. Sects that have added or subtracted from the Scriptures stand aloof from those who accept only what is in God's written revelation. And the same is true of those who have their own private interpretation of a particular doctrine and constantly harp on it. These things are principal causes of divisions. Pride of possessing more knowledge than another is the basis of isolationism and sectarianism.

Oral Tradition Versus the Scriptures

Churches and individuals often split up and differ because they regard their oral traditions as being of equal importance and authority with the Scriptures. But, when God gave the Ten Commandments, He did not commit them orally to Moses but engraved them on two stone tablets with His hand. When we pursue this matter still further, we find that God's law and prophecies, and all the history of God's dealings with His people and the heathen nations were invariably committed to writing.

It is said of the king who might be appointed over the Israelites that he should "write . . . a copy of this law in a book" (Deut. 17:18). To Jeremiah God said, "Write thee all the words that I have spoken unto thee in a book" (Jer. 30:2). When the Israelites returned from captivity, Ezra began to teach them the law of God—not from memory or from what had been traditionally handed down among them, but he "read in the book in the law of God distinctly, and gave the sense, and caused them to understand the reading" (Neh. 8:8).

The Jews were extremely jealous for the Word of God as against anything except what was written. This attitude was confirmed afterward by the Lord Jesus as He frequently rebuked the Pharisees for violating this rule by their traditions, which had encumbered and vitiated what had been written.

Of course, the Christian religion began, as was natural, in the teaching of man to man by word of mouth. But the Holy Spirit soon moved the same apostles who had preached orally to concentrate and gather together all the great points of such oral preaching in the Scriptures.

Today, generally speaking, Christendom is divided into two main branches: the churches such as the Roman Catholic and Eastern Orthodox, which place oral tradition on a par with the written Scriptures, and the Protestant churches, which accept the Scriptures as their sole authority, and place nothing alongside them or above them.

The word "tradition" in Greek is *paradosis,* meaning "something that is handed down." That may be done orally or in writing. Thus, whenever we come across the word "tradition" in the New Testament, we need to understand whether it refers to oral or written tradition. For instance, in I Corinthians 15:3, Paul says, "I have delivered unto you." The word is *paredooka,* the verbal form of *paradosis.* Thus he is saying, "I have made a tradition to you . . . that Christ died for our sins."

And in I Corinthians 11:2 Paul says, "I will praise you . . . that ye . . . keep the ordinances, as I delivered them unto you." The word translated "ordinances" is *paradoseis,* "traditions." He praises them for keeping "the traditions which I have handed down to you." And in II Thessalonians 2:15 he says, "Stand fast, and hold the traditions [*paradoseis*] which ye have been taught, whether by word, or our epistle." Here the word "traditions" refers to both oral and written teaching.

Unfortunately, however, the word "tradition" has taken on the ecclesiastical meaning of oral tradition only, in contradistinction to the written, which has assumed the name of "Scripture." Thus in actuality, Scripture is tradition, though it has lost the name; but "tradition" as understood and venerated today is not Scripture, because it lacks the essential addition of originally being set down in writing.

Before Scripture existed, there was oral tradition. Without such tradition, there could have been no Scripture at all. The Lord Jesus was crucified around A.D. 33. Matthew's Gospel was the first Scripture of the New Testament. We don't know exactly when it was written. Some set the date as late as A.D. 64, others as early as the year 38. Then the other Scriptures, both Gospels and Epistles, were added from time to time, as circumstances called for them, down to the close of the first century.

Therefore there was a period of from five to twenty years when there was no Scripture at all, as far as the New Testament was concerned. And then only one Gospel circulated among a very scanty number of Hebrew Christians. Christianity in that comparatively brief period could only depend on that oral teaching, that remembrance of doctrines delivered by the preaching of the apostles, and handed about by word of mouth from one person to another. And this we call tradition, not to be confused with later "traditions" such as the writings of the church Fathers, the creeds of councils, etc.

There then developed concise creeds that could be easily memorized and repeated. But matters of such momentous importance as salvation could not be left to the uncertain and feeble authority of hearsay. Consider, for instance, what your religion would be if it were to depend only on the sermons that you hear. By the time a sermon was told by one person to another down the line, for perhaps twenty or a hundred times, it couldn't help being altered, either by subtraction or exaggeration.

And would it then be likely that God, who knows men and human hearts, would leave a matter of such importance as the salvation of the whole human race, which had to be made known over the face of the whole world, and among nations of endlessly different languages, and which was to endure as the good tidings of God—to the changing humors of an oral communication? Surely not.

No Other Gospel

In our study so far we have seen that in the Old Testament the Lord insisted on the safety of a written revelation of His Word. And in the New Testament the Apostle Paul commanded that no one should think above what is written. The reason for this, of course, is that wrong behavior could be justified by unacceptable oral tradition. This may have been the case in the Corinthian church, to which Paul addressed this command. A church or an individual may seek to justify certain doctrines that are not grounded in the Scriptures by appealing to oral tradition.

But certain fundamental truths must be remembered in this regard:

1) That there could be no difference whatever between what the Scriptures record and the previously existing sacred traditions. They were one

and the same thing. The Scriptures could not contain one item more, and certainly not one item less, which was necessary to salvation, than had previously been circulated among the early Christians in the shape of creeds or summaries of faith.

2) These Scriptures could not, since inspired by the Holy Spirit, contain anything that might have been done subsequent to their publication. Therefore, if we should find a tradition asserted now by any Christians as being essential to salvation, which is not in Scripture also, we know that it must have been invented later than the apostolic age. But if we find a tradition that agrees with Scripture, or is contained in Scripture, or may be gathered out of Scripture, we may freely embrace that tradition. But we do so now because Scripture confirms and establishes it, and not because it confirms and establishes Scripture.

3) The very fact that the traditions were committed to Scripture at all does away with any supposition that traditional teaching is still left among Christians as being vital to their salvation. Otherwise why would God command His apostles, and inspire them by His Holy Spirit, to record the words and actions of Christ in writing, if some of the traditions, as previously existing, had still been necessary for them to believe in order to be saved? We might as well have been left even to this day without any Scripture at all, for there would be no advantage in it, or benefit to be derived from it. Therefore traditions cease to be necessary to salvation by the mere fact of there being any Scripture at all.

Think of it this way: Certain things were delivered by oral teaching during the life of Christ, and proclaimed by His apostles. It is impossible to suppose that Christ and His apostles could have taught an imperfect system of faith, or could have preached a Gospel that was not sufficient for salvation. All that was required to be taught was taught. Then, when this truth was in danger of being changed, mutilated, or added to because of the passage of time, or by the imperfect transmission of human channels of communication, God directed holy men, moved by His Holy Spirit, to write down all that had been said and done that was necessary for salvation.

Note that not all that was said and done was recorded. Many sayings and miracles of Christ were left unwritten, as John himself testifies in the last verse of his Gospel: "And there are also many other things which Jesus did, the which, if they should be written every one, I suppose that even the world itself could not contain the books that should be written" (John 21:25).

This is what we should understand in the great controversy that exists between the churches that believe in the Scriptures only and those that believe the Scriptures must be complemented by oral tradition. We freely admit that many things were said and done by the Lord Jesus that are not in Scripture, but we do not allow that any of these things were necessary for salvation. What was the principle of selection? "But these are written, that ye might believe that Jesus is the Christ, the Son of God; and that believing ye might have life through his name" (John 20:31). The principle of selection was this: "that ye might believe that Jesus is the Christ." The selection gives you all that you require; it is needless to give you more. If there had been anything further that was required "that . . . ye might have life through his name," it would have been recorded.

We dare say that the Apostle Paul even excludes his own teaching as something the Corinthians should accept if it should prove contrary to the teaching of the Lord Jesus Christ. He makes this plain in Galatians 1:8: "But though we, or an angel from heaven, preach any other gospel unto you than that which we have preached unto you, let him be accursed." (See also I Timothy 6:3, 4.)

(See *Lecture-Sermons,* by Rev. William J. E. Bennett, pp. 47-72.)

> Against this sea-swept Rock
>   Ten thousand storms their will
> Of foam and rage have wildly spent;
>   It lifts its calm face still.
>
> It standeth and will stand,
>   With neither change nor age,
> The Word of majesty and light,
>   The Church's heritage.
>   —Horatius Bonar

Is the Written Word of God Sufficient for Salvation?

God is very explicit about the finality of His Word. In Deuteronomy 4:2 He says, "Ye shall not add unto the word which I command you, neither shall ye diminish ought from it, that ye may keep the commandments of the Lord your God which I command you." This is a command against two evils, that of adding to and that of subtracting from the Word of God—the Word that was first spoken and then written.

"But," someone might say, "wasn't anything ever added to these words of the commandments of the Lord?" Of course there was, including the writings of the prophets, the Psalms, and other Old Testament books, and then the New Testament. Does that mean these are not valid? Of course not. What God prohibited was purely human additions to the Divine Word. The Jews looked upon the rest of the Old Testament as God's expansion of the Law (Torah).

What are we to understand by "adding" to God's Word? Bringing in heathen superstitions, or forms of worship different from those commanded. And what is meant by "diminishing from" God's Word? Neglecting some duty, or leaving out some observance, commanded in it.

What is the object of keeping God's Word without addition or subtraction? That people may fulfill all God's commandments as He originally gave them. How could adding prevent this? By putting human commands on a level with God's, thus causing confusion and giving wrong ideas and false authority. How would diminishing prevent this? By concealing from the people important requirements of God. And what does the last part of the text teach us as to our duty? That we are bound to carry out all that God requires of us. What temptation does our text guard us against? The temptation of taking part of God's will for the whole.

Many students of the Bible are confused nowadays about a group of books included in some Bibles called the Apocrypha, which means "the hidden ones (or books)." These books were written by the Jews in the period between the Old and New Testaments. They are rejected by Protestantism as not part of the Canonical Scriptures. These books were not contained in the Bible of the Jews from whom we received the Old Testament. The Apocrypha was first included as part of Scripture at the Council of Trent in 1547. (See *The 100th Text of the Society for Irish Church Missions,* a manual of theology by the Rev. T. C. Hammond, pp. 326-8.)

Those who believe that the Scripture is incomplete without the unwritten oral tradition of the Church point to John 21:25, "And there are also many other things which Jesus did, the which, if they should be written every one, I suppose that even the world itself could not contain the books that should be written." So the contention runs: "Why reject the words of Christ that are unwritten? Might there not have been among them many important points of instruction and discipline that our Lord commended to the keeping of His Church?"

Of course, we cannot prove that there were not; so, then, the objector would go on to say, "Not only might there have been, but when you consider other parts of Scripture, it is very probable, indeed, that there were. For instance, Paul in writing to the Corinthians praised them for keeping 'the traditions (ordinances) as I delivered them to you' (I Cor. 11:2). And to Timothy he says, 'Hold fast the form of sound words, which thou hast of me' (II Tim. 1:13)." And the objector would conclude, "Scripture, therefore, seems to say that the things which the evangelist and others left unwritten might be of equal authority with Scripture itself."

Our answer to this would be that some traditions may indeed be valid. No one is denying the fact that the Lord Jesus Christ gave many instructions to His disciples that were not written. We do not have everything He said in the Scriptures. It is humanly impossible that this should be so, as John said. But what we are saying is that those things that were not written are not necessary for our salvation, and that what has been written is sufficient unto salvation. Otherwise God would have been doing something quite useless in inspiring holy men to produce a written record that was insufficient.

We are therefore prepared to concede many things unwritten, but nothing worthy to be believed as "necessary to salvation." We do not deny that tradition contains truths independent of and contrary to Scripture. All things necessary to salvation rest only on Scripture. It is interesting to note in this connection that many old so-called gospels that claim to contain other words and deeds of Jesus are so at variance with the New Testament that their claims are patently false.

(See *Lecture-Sermons,* by Rev. William J. E. Bennett, pp. 73-8.)

> We search the world for truth, we cull
> The good, the pure, the beautiful,
> From graven stone and written scroll,
> From all old flower-fields of the soul;
> And, weary seekers of the best,
> We come back laden from our quest,
> To find that all the sages said
> Is in the Book our mothers read.
>
> —Author Unknown

The Sin of Exalting Christian Leaders

Although we have seen that Paul's injunction to the Corinthian Church in I Corinthians 4:6 should properly read, "not to think of things above that which is written," instead of not to think of "men" in this way, it can properly be applied to men also, in a secondary sense. Paul was deeply concerned about the divisions and factions in the Corinthian Church, caused by their exalting of one leader over another. And he proceeds in masterly fashion to correct this.

But the Church is made up of individuals, and only as individuals are corrected can the Church as a corporate entity be made whole. So Paul sets out to deal with each individual.

In the middle of I Corinthians 4:6 we find the telic conjunction *hina,* "so that": *"So that* ye might

40

learn in us not to think of men above that which is written; *so that* no one of you be puffed up for one against another." What does this signify? Paul is saying in effect, "I want to admonish each one of you as an individual, first of all not to go beyond what is written; stick to the Scriptures; for only thus can you be guided aright as an individual. And in the second place, don't let pride cause you to think that your leader is superior to someone else."

The principle Paul was stressing is that what each individual is, the local church is. The Corinthians approved of one apostle and disliked another. In thus setting themselves as judges, they were actually enhancing their individual self-importance.

Now, why does Paul connect the Scriptures with their opinions of men? Because the Scriptures do definitely teach what our relationship should be to those who minister the Gospel. The Corinthians forgot that even an apostle was only a minister by whom the faith was propagated. In their minds they constituted him as their own party leader. They were the ones who attributed importance to him, not recognizing his true value as being that which God made him—a minister and steward of the mysteries of God. Their support of a man had the subtle philosophy of asserting, "Here is what we have made you; this is the position to which we have elevated you. If it were not for our support, you wouldn't be what you are or where you are."

By their elevation of one man over another, the Corinthians were actually proclaiming their own importance in the support they were giving him. We see this in their tendency to treat him like a political leader whose electorate says to him, "You are what you are because of us. Therefore look how important we are." As Judge Harold Medina observed:

"Criticizing others is a dangerous thing, not so much because you may be making mistakes about them, but because you may be revealing the truths about yourself." And this holds true about praising men also.

A pastor, just before presenting a visiting minister to his congregation, prayed, "O Lord, blot him out so we can see only Jesus!" Wouldn't that be an appropriate prayer for each one of us? Esteem your minister as one who brings you closer to Christ and makes the Bible a book to be loved and obeyed. But don't puff up your minister, or yourself for belonging to him and what you consider "his party" in the church.

The Apostle Paul seeks to counteract such a spirit by asking one probing question after another, the answers to which were self-evident. We shall examine these questions in detail a bit later. Paul uses the same method in I Corinthians 1:13: "Is Christ divided? was Paul crucified for you? or were ye baptized in the name of Paul?" Naturally such questions are meant to strip the Corinthians of their "puffery" in attributing more value to an individual than the Scriptures permit. They thought they had the right to introduce new situations that would make them innovators of unquestioned authority.

Christian, watch yourself, lest you begin to think you know better than anyone else what ought to be done in the church, so that everyone should listen to you and follow your advice. You may find yourself in the humiliating position of being rebuked by a Higher Authority, God Himself, as His Holy Spirit speaks to you through the Scriptures.

It is said that Billie Burke, the Hollywood actress, was enjoying a transatlantic ocean voyage when she noticed that a man at the next table was suffering from a bad cold.

"Uncomfortable?" she asked sympathetically. The man nodded.

"I'll tell you what to do for it," she offered. "Go back to your stateroom and drink a lot of orange juice. Take five aspirin tablets. Cover yourself with all the blankets you can find. Sweat the cold out. I know what I'm talking about. I'm Billie Burke of Hollywood."

The man smiled warmly and said, "Thanks. I'm Dr. Mayo of the Mayo Clinic!"

Oh, these self-proclaimed experts who ride on an interpretative tangent and play a one-chord spiritual instrument! Lord, deliver us from believing that all the solutions rest in our own simplistic formulas, or in one man whom we believe to have all the answers. Deliver us from elevating anyone to such a degree that both Christ and His Word are obscured. Let us respect and honor Thy faithful ministers as we ought, but let us reserve our highest love, veneration, and loyalty for Thee.

Humility in Action

Admonitions to specific individuals and churches in Scripture, although they may be occasioned by a local situation, often have a wider application, for they address themselves to human nature. Thus, what the Apostle Paul has to say to the church at Corinth may be applied to the churches today. Are we any better than the Corinthian Christians? Are we less or more divided than they? Are we, like them, introducing new attitudes or even doctrines above what is written in Scripture?

Many churches today, sad to say, seem very much imbued with the spirit of the Corinthian church. One leader looks down upon another. And those who follow a particular leader sometimes refuse to have fellowship with those who follow another, as they consider them beneath them. Pride is the cause of such divisions in the Church. But the saddest thing of all is the ease and cleverness with which we try to justify the pride of our factionalism.

There are probably two leading objections to cultivating the humility that would provide the remedy for factionalism. In the first place, we don't want the humility that we think will compromise our sincerity and moral stature. We say in effect, "I believe something or in somebody, and therefore I must take a stand. If for the sake of humility I suppress my support, I am being insincere."

True enough, if that's what you think humility demands. But this is a false notion of humility. Those who entertain such a notion take humility to be something dramatic and unreal, a pretense put on for an occasion, instead of an attitude dictated by sincere feelings and conviction. This is not true humility, however. The humility we need is not a pretense, a winking at truth, but essentially the recognition of truth.

Just how does true humility manifest itself? It involves the taking, in act and word and thought, that low estimate of ourselves that is the true one—as God sees us and reveals it to us in Scripture. If we do not seriously think that such an estimate is the true one, it is only because we have never taken a hard look at ourselves as we really are. We have yet to learn our real relationship to the One to whom we owe our existence, or to recognize the weakness that impairs our moral force, and the evil that clings to us within.

In the meantime, we feel it is better not to pretend that we have done so; while it is certain that such pretense, if we should be guilty of it, would not be rightly termed humility. Christian humility, if it is genuine, is never exercised at the expense of truth, but as a result of the correct estimate of ourselves and the religious leader whom we may have elevated above what the Scriptures permit.

The second objection that may be advanced for failure to cultivate humility is the notion that it is something dramatic and fictitious, and therefore involves some loss of moral strength. This is true only if the humility we refer to is false, for moral force is vitiated by every form of untruthfulness. Genuine humility, however, is in its essence the planting of our feet upon the hard rock of truth and fact, often at great cost to our pride. To confess ignorance or wrong, to admit incapacity when it would be useful to be thought capable, to decline a reputation to which we have no right—these things, and others of the same kind, are humility in action. If we are weak, sinful, corrupt, it is better to learn and to feel the true state of the case than to live in a fool's paradise.

How foolish a country would be to go to war with a false estimate of its own strength. Every man is the stronger for knowing the worst he can know about himself, and for acting on this knowledge. If Godfearing men such as David and Paul used language about themselves that seems to any of us exaggerated in the excess of its self-depreciation (as in Psalm 51:1-3 and I Corinthians 15:9), this is because they saw much more evil than we do. To them such language was only the sober representation of a plain fact. These great servants of God were not dazzled by any of the inherited or acquired status symbols that hide from so many of us our real selves, and which the Apostle Paul in I Corinthians 4:6 is so determined to strip off from us.

A government official in India who was engaged in irrigation work came to the owner of a field and offered to make it fruitful, to which the owner answered. "You needn't attempt to do anything with my field; it is barren and will produce nothing." The official replied, "I can make your field richly fruitful if only it lies low enough." He meant that a lowland would be much easier to irrigate than higher ground.

If you and I are willing to accept God's estimate of us as revealed in Scripture—as fallible, weak, and unfruitful apart from His enabling grace in Christ—He can fill us with the living water that will bring forth fruit.

One of the last messages of a great philanthropist was, "Tell my younger brethren that they may be too big for God to use them, but they cannot be too small."

The Mystery
of Life's Inequalities

"For who maketh thee to differ from another? and what hast thou that thou didst not receive? now if thou didst receive it, why dost thou glory as if thou hadst not received it?" (I Cor. 4:7).

Equality: A Utopian Dream?

The Declaration of Independence affirms: "We hold these truths to be self-evident, that all men are created equal, that they are endowed by their Creator with certain inalienable rights, that among these are Life, Liberty, and the Pursuit of Happiness."

Most men believe in equality. The Declaration of Independence proclaims this in no uncertain terms. The question, however, is what is meant by the term "equality." The equality of which the Declaration of Independence speaks is an equality of rights, not of personal endowments. The idealist, on the other hand, believes in an equality that would have created all men with equal abilities, opportunities, and material possessions. He frowns at the injustice of any form of inequality. He despises the employer who doesn't treat everyone equally. He even questions a God who disperses His gifts unequally.

And yet none of us can be so naive as not to realize that we live in a world of inequalities. We have different innate intelligences. Though we have all been created with pretty much the same physical equipment, the intensity of our strength differs. Our environments differ. We possess individual and differing abilities. And we can only conclude that God made us that way, whether we can understand it or not. It's one of those unfathomable mysteries that we must accept as a fact and come to terms with.

No two snowflakes, no two blades of grass, no two animals, no two human countenances, exactly correspond with each other. God could have made everything uniform within its kind, but He didn't. His creation is characterized by variety.

What Paul suggests through his epistles is that the Author of differences between man and man is the infinitely wise and good God. Judging as sinful men, though we may not like it, and may even think we could have done better in God's place, we know there's nothing we can do to improve on the work of our Creator. It's a utopian dream to conclude that complete equality in all things would have been preferable. We just don't know. Nor will God permit our experimentation in such a situation in our present state of being and environment. Our nature is fallen and our environment is geared to such a fallen nature. Some day, with the complete redemption of our being and environment, this may become possible.

Paul wanted to correct the attitudes of the Corinthians in esteeming one servant of God more highly than another. Human esteem differs because people differ. We tend to appreciate and admire one whom we regard as a capable preacher. We become critical toward one whom we regard as an average or poor one. The fact that our appreciation of people varies is proof that people are different. But who is it that makes them different as far as their essential endowments are concerned? It is God.

In I Corinthians 4:7 Paul asks the question, "Who maketh thee to differ from another? and what hast thou that thou didst not receive?" "Who" and "what"? There is a giver behind every gift. Thus the two questions are practically one, for everything ultimately comes from God—including the differences that make human lives unequal. These differences are as much a part of His handiwork as anything else in the world of being. Therefore, to quarrel with them, or to make them the occasion of rivalry with and estrangement from others, is to declare war upon the wisdom and purpose of the Great Creator.

Variety and difference in our world are not the result of chance. They are not the fatal outcome of the inter-operation of self-existent matter and force molded by some self-existent system of complex laws. It is God who has made us, and not we ourselves (see Ps. 100:3). And it is certainly not that indefinite abstraction that men call "nature."

What we are called upon to do is to note the differences that separate us as human beings, accept them as the framework within which we have to work, and examine how these refer to the will and power and wisdom of God. These differences can be classified first as external circumstances, second as personal endowments, and third as spiritual opportunities. We shall take these up in separate studies.

What we must do now is to allow God to be God in our thinking, and to acknowledge that He is all-wise, all-knowing, all-good.

John Greenleaf Whittier came to terms with this when he wrote:

I have no answer, for myself or thee,
Save that I learned beside my mother's knee:
"All is of God that is, and is to be;
And God is good." Let this suffice us still,
Resting in childlike trust upon His will
Who moves to His great ends unthwarted by
the ill.

"Take comfort, and recollect however little you and I may know, God knows; He knows Himself and you and me and all things; and His mercy is over all His works."—Charles Kingsley.

Differences in Our External Circumstances: Can They Be Helped?

Human society is full of inequalities—often quite glaring. Some people are wealthy, some are starving; some have great influence, others are regarded as nobodies. There are inequalities of education, social position, and opportunities. And these often cause great dissatisfaction and ferment between the haves and have-nots.

We may blame the spirit of injustice among men, tradition, misgovernment, our social and economic systems, the selfishness of the rich, and the chronic inertia of the poor. But whatever or whomever we may blame for the inequalities of human circumstances, we are ultimately forced back on the conclusion that it is God Himself who makes one man to differ from another. He makes men differ originally in their productive powers, and this, in part, is responsible for the unequal distribution of wealth and the disparity in men's social position.

It follows from this that projects for reconstructing society on the basis of an equal distribution of property of whatever kind are in conflict with the original facts of human nature, that is to say, with what was ordained by the will of God. For instance, suppose you were to divide all the land equally among the inhabitants of a nation. You'd soon find out that a man capable of cultivating 1,000 acres was wasting his ability on the ten acres or so allotted to everybody, while a person given ten acres might be found incapable of handling even that little. No human theory or law can affect this original inequality of productive power in men, which is the main and permanent cause of differences in wealth and social position. Nature and fact would assert themselves against utopian theory.

Don't get me wrong. I'm not upholding privilege against right, wealth against poverty, the few against the many, or that which has been against that which ought to be. Nor am I trying to excuse wrong by making God responsible for it. This has been the contention of communism, causing it to reject God and religion. Since, it is maintained, God is responsible for these inequalities, we don't want anything to do with such a God.

The Christian points in reply to the future, in which whatever comes short of the requirements of justice here will be perfectly and forever redressed. Those who misunderstand this attitude accuse us of promising "pie in the sky" at the cost of neglecting efforts to improve man's present lot. Christianity never says, however, that inequalities which involve moral wrong are to be acquiesced in here because they will be corrected hereafter. Moral wrongs must be corrected here and now, whenever possible.

But not all the differences of position, education, and income in themselves involve moral wrong. The fact that you or I may occupy a so-called higher social position than someone else doesn't necessarily classify us as immoral, thus making us automatically responsible for the lower social position of another. Nor is the person who has remained on the lower rungs of the social or economic ladder necessarily to be held morally culpable for his non-advancement.

It is sinful, however, for us as Christians to shut our eyes to the need of others. We are bound to do everything in our power to lessen the general inequalities of life. Our charities ought to throw bridges over the gulfs that separate classes. Christianity breeds a spirit of self-sacrifice that results in the voluntary abandonment of wealth and station for the sake of others, out of devotion to Jesus Christ, who, "though he was rich, yet for your sakes he became poor, that ye through his poverty might be rich" (II Cor. 8:9).

But it is inevitably true that, when all that can be done in this direction has been done, great inequalities in men's outward circumstances will and must remain, because they are due to inherited differences of personal capacity. And this is so because, in making us, our Creator has willed that one man should widely differ from another. Inequalities of circumstances are part and parcel of inequalities in personal endowments, and these are really beyond our control.

In I Corinthians 4:7 Paul says that those who have been more privileged have no reason to be proud, as though they were somehow responsible for their more fortunate lot. Scripture tells us that men are like clay in the potter's hands, God being the Potter, of course. Can a beautiful clay vase boast itself against a common pot, saying, "I am much finer than you and therefore worthy of praise"? As the vase contributed nothing toward its beauty, so man contributes nothing to his inherent individual make-up. True, he can develop himself, but only to the extent of "what he has been made to be in his real self."

In fact, those who have received more from God than others should not be proud, but acknowledge they are more in debt to Him for the bounty He has bestowed on them. Why should one man boast that he is deeper in debt than another? Let's regard our endowments as a trust to be used for the glory of God and the good of our fellow men.

How to Regard Inequalities Due to Differences in Personal Endowments

Men differ in the physical, mental, and other qualities with which God has sent them into the world. No two men are exactly equal even in the possession of a single faculty or talent. School teachers are keen observers of such inequalities.

What has heredity to do with all this? In our endeavor to understand present behavior we must analyze an individual's ancestry. But this poses another question: Why should a given individual have this particular ancestry, which has shaped him into the physical and mental person we now see? In fact, why should there be any antecedents at all, or any effects, anything to be transmitted, or any law of type to govern its transmission?

These are indeed difficult questions to answer. In their presence, science is wisely silent. We must turn to the Bible for authoritative answers to them. To those who believe in God the Creator, who made us all, and each one of us exactly what we are, there can be no question as to the true source of natural ability. Handel, the composer of "The Messiah," gave eloquent testimony to this. On one occasion when his oratorio was superbly rendered by an orchestra, chorus, and soloists, the audience broke out in thunderous applause, while all eyes turned toward Handel. He, however, turned their attention from himself to his Creator, as he stood up and silently pointed heavenward. How salutary and humbling to recognize that what basically distinguishes us from others is a gift from God.

Someone once had the temerity to say what many of us are tempted to think: "I am a self-made man." A friend replied, "That certainly relieves God of an embarrassing responsibility." Anyone who regards himself as a self-made man should stop and think that he must have had some material to begin with. Where did his mind come from? He didn't choose the circumstances of his birth. He could have been born an idiot. Even if he became a distinguished athlete, it was God who gave him his body. The voice, eyesight, and physical coordination, to mention just a few of our physical attributes, are all gifts we have received from God; and only because He gave them to us could we develop them.

We have made great advances in our study of heredity and how it works, including how traits are transmitted. It is truly gracious of the Supreme Artist to have allowed us to see further into His workshop than our fathers did, and to discover some of the rules by which He conducts His work. But the work is none the less His because it is done by rules He allows us to observe. If every peculiarity of our minds and bodies could be accounted for by those of our ancestors, we would not be one bit less God's workmanship, each made to differ from others by a deliberate act of His will.

Now we come to the subject of inequalities in our spiritual advantages and opportunities. The words of the Apostle Paul, "Who maketh thee to differ from another? and what hast thou that thou didst not receive?'' were addressed to people who were proud of their spiritual leader and were boasting of him as well as their own spiritual superiority. The Corinthian Christian addressed by Paul believed himself to differ from his fellow Christians, not so much in social standing or intellectual culture, as more specifically in the possession of a higher degree of spirituality.

Paul didn't tell the Corinthian that the idea of his differing from another was a presumptuous absurdity. In fact, he attributed this difference basically to God Himself. If Apollos, for instance, had greater oratorical ability than Peter, that difference need not be concealed. Paul assumed that differences existed among preachers as well as followers. There was no reason to be proud of such differences, for the beginning of all spiritual life is the result of God's grace. Even the faith to receive the grace of God is a gift, as Paul points out so emphatically in Ephesians 2:8: ''For by grace are ye saved through faith; and that not of yourselves: it is the gift of God.''

However, you and I were born where we could hear the Gospel and receive the offer of salvation. But millions on this earth were not. Inequality of opportunity to hear that wonderful Gospel that changes men's eternal destiny raises many questions. Why should one person be born into a godly home, with all the opportunities of Christian example, and others not? If the differences of religious circumstances come from God, why? We just don't know. We can only be observers of such actions of God, not interpreters of them. We don't reject Him, however, because we can't fully understand Him, no more than a small child rejects his parents because their actions are often incomprehensible to him. Nor do we lament our lack of opportunities. God will judge us by what we do with the opportunities He gives us. And we to whom He has given the opportunity and privilege of receiving Christ must rush to share the knowledge of His grace with those who have not yet had the opportunity. For as Paul said, "I am debtor both to the Greeks, and to the Barbarians; both to the wise, and to the unwise" . . . and "Woe is unto me, if I preach not the gospel!" (Rom. 1:14, I Cor. 9:16).

Inequalities in Spiritual Endowments

If you will turn in your Bible to the 12th chapter of First Corinthians, you will see that spiritual gifts and opportunities are unequally distributed. "Now there are diversities of gifts, but the same Spirit." But the inequality of gifts, even of spiritual gifts, doesn't imply that God loves those individuals less to whom He gives less. He gives according to our capacity to receive. He withholds, as He bestows, in love.

God often imposes drawbacks and difficulties, when He sees that these are needed for the training and discipline of the thoughts, emotions, and will; so that underlying the great differences of spiritual advantage there is a much truer equality than we may think. As in a well-ordered state all are basically equal before the law, so in the Church all are basically equal before their Maker and Redeemer.

To be specific, we are equals in that we must all face the solemn moment of death. We are equal in that we shall all be judged relative to the gifts and opportunities we have enjoyed. We are equal in that all of us can be saved only one way, through the blood of Jesus Christ shed on the cross. And we are equals in that we have all received a trust from God. Some of us may have been entrusted with five talents, some two, others one. Some may have received the abilities of Paul, others of Apollos. But the Church, after all, is like a great almshouse, in which everybody is a pensioner, and in which the difference between the greatest and the smallest pensions disappears before the fact that all are equally indebted to a bounty on which none have any real claim. All that God gives us is wrapped up in the word "grace." We have nothing to do with winning it. We may cooperate with it; we may forfeit it by neglect; we may or may not have predispositions for receiving it. But in itself, it is, as its name implies, a free gift from God.

Is there anything that we have not received from God? Yes, there is. We all have it, but we can't blame God for giving it to us. It is the fatal product of our misused liberty. That is sin. God originally made man in His own image and likeness. But this meant that He created man with the original power of choice, even as He Himself had it. But God also had to set the consequences of the choices man would make. Man could choose whether to obey God or not, but he could not choose the consequences of his choice. Thus sin, and the will to sin, are not something we received from God, but simply a result of the choice to sin or not to sin.

Never blame God for your sin. You are right in ascribing to Him your freedom to choose; but when you stop to consider that privilege which distinguishes you from all the rest of creation, you will praise God for it rather than blame Him.

Dr. Pierce Harris, pastor of the First Methodist Church of Atlanta, Georgia, preached to some prisoners. One of the prisoners got up and introduced him to the others with these words: "Several years ago, two boys lived in a town in north Georgia. They went to the same school, played together and attended the same Sunday school. One dropped out of Sunday school and said that it was 'sissy stuff.' The other boy kept on going. One rejected Christ; the other accepted Him. The boy who rejected Christ is making this introduction today. The boy who accepted Christ is the honored preacher who will speak to us today!" Choice made the difference.

What should our attitude be as we see others possessing gifts that we do not possess and that we cannot acquire? Jealousy, resentment, and disparagement of others are all too often evidenced by the less-gifted in the Church. A man came up to Moody once and criticized him for the way he went about winning souls. Moody listened courteously and then asked, "How would you do it?" The man, taken aback, mumbled that he didn't do it. "Well," said Moody, "I prefer the way I do it to the way you don't do it."

We should thank the Lord that others can serve God in ways that we cannot. After all, the important thing is not what you and I as individuals can do, but what can be done for the Kingdom of God. Let's always look at the abilities of others as supplements to what little we can do, and praise God for the gifts He has given others. If no one cared who got the credit for services rendered to God, how much more might be accomplished for Him— and in the right spirit.

As we realize what God has given to us—the talents and abilities with which He has entrusted us—let's acquire a sense of urgent responsibility to use them for His glory. The more splendid the endowment the greater the possibility of its misuse. The higher the gift the more there is to be accounted for.

The realization that what men have was given by God ought to make us tender and sympathetic toward the less-gifted instead of haughty and contemptuous. And, toward the more highly gifted than we, our feeling should be one of delight and gratitude that they can accomplish what we cannot.

(See "Humility and Truth," in *Liddon's University Sermons, Second Series,* pp. 18-37.)

Material Progress at the Cost of Spiritual Compromise

"Now ye are full, now ye are rich, ye have reigned as kings without us: and I would to God ye did reign, that we also might reign with you" (I Cor. 4:8).

Present Satisfaction Versus Future Joy

One of the commonest pitfalls for a Christian is to be caught up in the spirit of the age, to live for the here and now. When a Christian believes that his full satisfaction is to be found in this world, he will tend to seek three things that man in his unregenerate state considers most important: physical satisfaction, the acquisition of wealth, and the power and prestige that enable him to rule over others. These are the cravings of the natural man, with which the Christian is all too often infected.

The Lord fully recognized this in the Beatitudes in Matthew 5:3-11 and Luke 6:20-24. But full satisfaction, riches, and rule over others are something He promises to the Christian in the world to come, not here. In this world, the Christian will often have to go without. "Blessed the hungering ones now: for they shall be filled" (Luke 6:21). Observe that the filling is future. "Blessed the sorrowing ones: for they shall be comforted" (Matt. 5:4). That's also in the future. "Blessed the meek: for they shall inherit the earth" (Matt. 5:5). That's future rulership over the earth.

The general tenor is that what the natural man craves and expects to enjoy fully here and now, the Christian either is deprived of because of the environment in which he lives, or voluntarily deprives himself of in order to serve God better.

"Already," Paul says to the carnal Corinthians, who were factional and critical even of apostolic authority, "you are filled to satiety." This was in contrast to the apostles themselves, as Paul tells them in verse 11: "Even unto this present hour we both hunger, and thirst, and are naked, and are buffeted, and have no certain dwellingplace." This is the contrast Paul draws between the pleasure-seeking Corinthian Christians and the apostles who were voluntarily depriving themselves for the sake of proclaiming the Gospel.

The Greek word *eedee* is very important. "Already" is a more correct translation than the "now" of the Authorized Version. It's repeated twice in verse 8: "Already" you are filled to satiety; "already" you grew rich. The apostle rebukes the Corinthians for having sought these things prematurely. You have sought and acquired already that which you have been promised as children of the Kingdom of the future, when the Lord returns in His rewarding glory.

The matter of seeking on earth that which the Lord has promised us in heaven is emphasized in Matthew 6, where He gives us the example of three individuals who were doing something in itself good, but with wrong motive. The first gave alms, not primarily to help the needy but to be seen and praised of men. The second prayed in public places, not primarily to be heard of God, but to be heard and commended for his piety by men. And the third fasted, not to invoke God's attention, but man's pity. In all three cases the Lord says these people got what they sought—the praise, the attention, the pity of men; but that's all they were going to get. The Greek verb used in Matthew 6:2, 5, and 16 is *apechousin,* "they have their reward in full." They need not look for a reward in heaven, since they sought it here and now from men. They already have it.

In the Beatitudes in Luke 6:20-26, the Lord contrasts the self-sacrificing Christian (verses 20-23) with the selfish Christian who seeks his full satisfaction here and now, to the detriment of his effective witness (verses 24-26). The whole section here is divided by the Greek word *pleen,* "but," which contrasts the two classes of Christians—those who seek pleasure, wealth, and fame on earth, and those who sacrifice them here to find them in heaven.

It was so in Corinth. In Luke 6:24 we find the same word *apechete* (*apechoo*) that is used in Matthew 6. "But woe unto you the rich! for you have in full your comfort." In Luke 6:21 the verb *apechete* is in the present tense, indicating "here and now, already," in contrast to the future of *chortastheesesthe* (you will be full), and *gelasete* (you will laugh), in the day that is coming. For the self-sacrificing Christian, the reward is future.

There is a story of an aged servant of the Lord who, on his death-bed, said, "It is true; it is all true." Someone asked, "Why do you keep saying that? What is all true?" The aged Christian said, "Well, although I have given up all my possessions to the poor, and although I have turned from the things of the world, yet I never could really believe those words, 'Whosoever giveth up father, or mother, or houses, or lands, for my name's sake shall . . . receive his full reward, and shall enter into life eternal,' but now that I am dying I have found it is true; it is all true.''

When a friend once wrote to Dr. Livingstone about the sacrifices he was making in spending his days among the savages of Central Africa, he made the spirited reply: ''Is that a sacrifice which brings its own best reward in healthful activity, in the consciousness of doing good, peace of mind, and the hope of a glorious destiny hereafter? Away with such a thought! I never made a sacrifice.'' May we, too, seek ''first the kingdom of God, and his righteousness,'' rather than our own selfish satisfaction.

Suffering Here but Reigning Hereafter

What I am about to say may come as an unpalatable truth to those Christians who have been caught up in the spirit of the age; but I do not believe a Christian can possibly experience all the satisfaction, wealth, and fame this life can offer without some compromise of principle. The Bible tells us that the Christian's full pleasure, wealth, and fame is future. Though a Christian is free to seek these things, he cannot have his cake and eat it too. In that day of which the Apostle Paul spoke so eloquently in the 3rd chapter of I Corinthians, when Christ comes to distribute His rewards, He will say to those who sought a full measure of pleasure, wealth, and fame on earth, ''You have already had your reward in full.''

The Greek word Paul uses to demonstrate ''fullness to satiety'' is *kekoresmenoi*, from *korennumi*. It is evident from the context that this implies physical food rather than spiritual, and by extension satisfaction that comes from physical things, that is, pleasure to the full. This same verb occurs in Acts 27:38, in the account of the shipwreck in which Paul and 276 others were involved. Paul encouraged them to eat. And then, "when they had eaten enough [*koresthentes*], they lightened the ship, and cast out the wheat into the sea."

That Paul was referring to satiety with physical food, rather than the spiritual food that lexicographers Arndt and Gingrich mistakenly assume this statement to mean, is proven by the verses that follow, which deal with the physical privations of the disciples: "Even unto this present hour we both hunger, and thirst, and are naked, and are buffeted, and have no certain dwellingplace; and labour, working with our hands: being reviled, we bless; being persecuted, we suffer it" (I Cor. 4:11, 12).

The riches referred to in the second clause of verse 8 must also refer to physical wealth in contrast to the apostolic plight described in verses 11 and 12: "We go hungry, we go thirsty, and we are naked." That's all physical. These Corinthians constituted the haughty Christians who were priding themselves on their physical possessions. Their seeking such material satisfactions was unwarranted in view of their spiritual riches in Christ of which Paul spoke to Corinthian Christians in general in I Corinthians 1:5: "That in every thing ye are enriched by him [or 'in him,' i.e., Christ, as the Greek has it], in all utterance, and in all knowledge." That's positional enrichment. We are rich spiritually by virtue of the fact that we are "in Christ." This kind of wealth never produces pride, for we realize that all we are and have is from Christ. To seek to become rich materially, at the expense of our spiritual wealth, is unwarranted and dangerous. It's possible, but it's a deplorable snare for a Christian to fall into.

The two verbs used in I Corinthians 1:5 and 4:8 are somewhat different. In the first instance, where Paul is referring to their positional spiritual enrichment in Christ, he says *eploutistheete* (*ploutizoo*), which is the second person plural, first aorist, in the passive voice, meaning, You were enriched by someone other than yourselves, and that, of course, is God. But in I Corinthians 4:8 the verb is *eplouteesate,* which is the second person plural, first aorist indicative, of the verb *plouteoo,* which means "to become rich," on your own. Christ makes us spiritually rich, but we become materially rich on our own. Already, Paul says, you have become, or you grew, rich on your own. He implies that neither he nor any other apostle had helped them to achieve this material enrichment.

This disclaimer is further sustained by what Paul states in the third clause of verse 8: "Without us you reigned." "Without us" in Greek is *chooris heemoon,* which actually means "without our participation." Paul uses the aorist tense in an ingressive form to indicate the entrance upon a condition: "You are still reigning," in other words, "You are full, you are rich, you are ruling." Actually the word "reign" (*basileuoo*) is used with the meaning of ruling over others, referring to fame. This is in contrast to the future role of the Christians when they shall reign with Christ (see II Tim. 2:12). Again it implies premature seeking in the physical world of something the Lord has promised for the world to come.

Paul is quick to point out how deceived the Corinthians were in thinking they were really ruling in this world. "And would that you did rule," he says, "and continue to rule, so that we too might reign with you." The Greek verb *ophelon,* in the past tense, indicative mood, as here, expresses a wish that is, at the same time, impossible of attainment (see Rev. 3:15). To rule over the world here and now is impossible, although we wish it were true, especially as we suffer so much for Christ's sake in this evil environment. Paul was writing to the Corinthians from Ephesus, where he was greatly persecuted. Read the 19th chapter of Acts and see what he went through at the hands of the devotees of the Ephesian goddess Diana. "I wish it were possible for you really to rule; and then there might be a chance for us to rule with your help," Paul says in effect. But that day will only come when we shall live and reign with Christ in His Kingdom.

The Least Among Men, the Greatest before God

"For I think that God hath set forth us the apostles last, as it were appointed to death: for we are made a spectacle unto the world, and to angels, and to men" (I Cor. 4:9).

Making the Higher Choice

What should be the attitude of the Christian toward seeking physical pleasure, material wealth, and worldly fame? In I Corinthians 4:8, the Apostle Paul told the Corinthian Christians that they had enjoyed all these things, but that these were not the recompense that comes to faithful believers. They had sought that which earth bestows and had received it. That's the privilege of both unbeliever and believer. A believer, however, has the choice of forfeiting pleasure, wealth, and fame for that higher reward that will be his in heaven. The Corinthian Christians had made their decision—to eat their cake here on earth, so to speak—an attitude Paul wants to correct in them.

In verse 9, however, Paul proceeded to state the apostolic position, the choice which he and the other apostles had made. "For I think that God hath set forth us the apostles last. . . ." That is in contrast to you Corinthians, who have chosen to be first here on earth.

Not everyone is willing to accept this choice, however. A young man who was trying to establish himself as a peach grower had worked hard, and invested all his money in a peach orchard. It blossomed wonderfully, but then came a killing frost. He didn't go to church the next Sunday, nor the next, nor the next. His minister went to see him to discover the reason. The young fellow exclaimed, "I'm not coming any more. Do you think I can worship a God who cares for me so little that He would let a frost kill all my peaches?"

The old minister looked at him a few moments in silence, then said kindly, "God loves you better than He does your peaches. He knows that while peaches do better without frosts, it is impossible to grow the best men without frosts. His object is to grow men, not peaches." We are sometimes so concerned about our material possessions that we fail to realize that setting our heart upon them can stunt our spiritual development. God often has to open our eyes to life's real values by taking from us its lesser ones.

Paul speaks here as a representative of the apostolic group. "For I think that God hath set forth *us*. . . ." He was speaking primarily of the apostles, but there is also a secondary reference to all the blessed whom God indwells and who have chosen a life of sacrifice instead of a life of abundance and luxury. Some Christians choose all they can get on earth, and others prefer to place their treasures where they can enjoy them not only for threescore years and ten but for eternity.

The implication here, however, is that, as an

apostle or servant of Christ, you ought to belong to the group of sacrificing Christians—either that, or not profess to be an apostle or servant of Christ at all. If the minister, the missionary, the Christian worker, does not live as if heaven were his permanent home, he might as well not preach or teach others. It is a serious and awesome responsibility to be a servant of Jesus Christ. You have to have the mind of Christ and be willing to live as He did, if you want others to listen to you and become Christlike.

A wealthy university graduate chose to live frugally in a single room, cooking his own meals. As a result he was able to give two million dollars to foreign missions. In explanation of his choice he wrote these words: "Gladly would I make the floor my bed, a box my chair, and another box my table, rather than that men should perish for want of knowledge of Christ." I am not suggesting that all Christians are called upon to forfeit the normal comforts of life; only that when God calls them to a life of sacrifice they be willing to leave all and follow Him.

Some missionaries were fleeing for their lives from pursuing bandits. They huddled together in an old abandoned building. It was filthy and vermin-ridden. Among the missionaries were Archibald Glover and his family. After a wretched night, little five-year-old Hendley Glover said, "Daddy, I think Jesus must have slept in a place like this when He had nowhere to go." "Yes, my boy, I think it very likely," answered Archibald.

"Then," said little Hendley, "we ought to be glad to be like Jesus, and suffer for Him."

There is a beautiful contrast between verses 8 and 9. All the verbs in verse 8 are in the aorist tense, indicating that the pleasure, wealth, and fame enjoyed by the Corinthians were their personal achievement. "You became full to satiety, you enriched yourselves, you became kings." This was all their own accomplishment. But in verse 9 the subject of the verb is God. "For I think that *God* hath set forth us the apostles last."

The verb *apedeixen,* "hath set forth," has God as its subject and the apostles as its object. The condition in which the apostles were found was not the result of any default on their part or the sheer fate of circumstances. It was the guiding hand of God. This verse is in full agreement with the truth the same apostle stresses in Romans 8:28: "And we know that all things work together for good to them that love God, to them who are the called according to his purpose."

"The Last Shall Be First"

Did you ever study plane geometry in school? If so, you know that, for every given theorem, you had to prove the truth of your postulate. And when you had proven it, you wrote QED at the end, meaning that you had demonstrated it, and it was so.

That's the significance of the Greek verb *apedeixen,* from *apodeiknumi,* "attest, set forth," in I Corinthians 4:9. It is akin to "he proved." The Lord had told His disciples that they would be persecuted and be considered the very offscouring of the earth. And now they were in the fray of the battle, in the situation predicted. Therefore in them God demonstrated what He set out to prove, that they would last through the predicted circumstances. On the forehead of the disciples could be written QED, *apodeixis,* "proof." They were proven by God, they lasted through.

If steel is to be used in a reliable manner, it must be tested and proven. So must the servant of Christ. Someone describes his visit to a steel mill as follows: "All around me were little partitions and compartments. Steel had been tested to the limit, and marked with figures that showed its breaking point. Some pieces had been twisted until they broke, and the strength of torsion was marked on them. Some had been stretched to the breaking point, and their tensile strength indicated. Some had been compressed to the crushing point and also marked. The supervisor of the steel mill knew just what these pieces of steel would stand under the strain. He knew just what they would bear if placed in a great ship, building, or bridge. He knew because the testing room revealed it."

It is often so with us as God's children. God doesn't want us to be like vases of glass or porcelain. He doesn't want us to be hothouse plants, but stormbeaten oaks; not sand dunes, driven with every gust of wind, but granite rocks withstanding the fiercest storms. To make us strong He must bring us into His testing room of suffering. Better the storm waters with Christ than the smooth waters without Him.

If you were to visit Paris, you could see the statues of two men, both named Louis. The first is of Louis XIV, France's absolute monarch, who is remembered today chiefly for his exclamation, "I am the State." He represents one of the supreme achievements of greatness through power. His philosophy of life was that the whole nation and the world, insofar as he could compel it, should serve him.

A few blocks away is a less pretentious statue. There is no uniform on this figure carved in stone, no badge of office, no sword, no crown. It is a memorial to Louis Pasteur, the servant of humanity and servant of God. His life of unselfish, devoted research conferred immeasurable benefits upon all humanity in all the years to come through overcoming disease and suffering.

The statue of the monarch is nothing more than a piece of sculpture; the statue of Pasteur is a shrine, where pilgrims from all over the world pay grateful homage. It is the uncrowned servant of mankind who wears the real crown of men's love and honor. As you look back, would you rather be remembered as Louis XIV who became supreme ruler of France and now has just a statue to commemorate him, or Louis Pasteur who is now crowned as an apostle of mercy? God's Word enjoins us not to be affected by the glamor of the moment but rather by the judgment of eternity.

If you as a Christian have the capacity for occupying a much higher rung on the social, economic, or political ladder, but for the sake of Christ are occupying a lowly place, it may sometimes cause you a momentary pang of regret. However, there is no greater satisfaction than temporarily to occupy the last place for Christ's sake, out of love for Him who occupied the lowest place for you. He relinquished the glory of heaven to come down to earth as a helpless Babe, born in a stable, growing up as a carpenter by trade, being rejected and vilified by those whom He offered the gift of eternal life, and finally dying on a cross, the sinless One paying the penalty for the sins of mankind.

I can well imagine how Peter felt when he said to Jesus, "Behold, we have forsaken all, and followed thee; what shall we have therefore?" (Matt. 19:27). Study Jesus' answer carefully: "Verily I say unto you, That ye which have followed me, in the regeneration when the Son of man shall sit in the throne of his glory, ye also shall sit upon the twelve thrones, judging the twelve tribes of Israel.

And every one that hath forsaken houses, or brethren, or sisters, or father, or mother, or wife, or children, or lands, for my name's sake, shall receive an hundredfold, and inherit everlasting life. But many that are first shall be last; and the last shall be first" (vv. 28-30).

The lowly position, the last place, is occupied only temporarily, while the first place will be occupied forever. It's worth sacrificing earth's honors and rewards for the joy that is set before us.

The Willingness to Risk Our Lives for Christ

In this world, we normally congratulate those who have achieved some degree of success and fame in their chosen field. But the Bible tells us that God sees not as man sees. His values are often far different from human values. The Apostle Paul caught a vision of this when he enumerated what God had proved Christ's disciples to be, as they labored for Him.

1) They were at the bottom of the social ladder—last—*eschatous*. That's the Greek word from which we get "eschatology," the study of last things. This was in contrast to what the carnal or immature Christians in Corinth had been able to achieve for themselves: satiety, riches, and power or fame. While they were enjoying all this, God permitted the consecrated apostles to be at the bottom of the scale of pleasure, wealth, and fame. But to be where God places and proves you is far better than any elevated position you yourself could achieve. If you are the last, you have nothing to pride yourself on except the One who put you there.

2) They were "sentenced to die." The Greek expression is *hoos epithanatious,* as if you were condemned to die at any moment, or on the verge of death. This doesn't mean that any of the apostles to

whom Paul refers had at that time been actually tried in court and were awaiting their execution date. It refers rather to the readiness of an apostle or servant of Christ to die at any time for His sake.

A small party of missionaries were invited to go to Tibet at a time when missionary activity was forbidden there. They were told their task was to help stem the tide of a plague that was raging out of control. When the plague was over, the government asked the missionaries to leave. But these servants of Christ felt a responsibility to minister to the souls of the Tibetans as well as to their bodies. The authorities threatened to kill them, but the fear of death did not deter them from their purpose. They stayed on.

One night the Tibetans encircled their house with flaming torches. They began dancing around in a wide circle, ever diminishing in size seeking to achieve their aim of setting the place ablaze. The missionaries fell to their knees in prayer, and became so intent as the wild chanting came closer that they never realized it had ceased. When they arose, the mob had dispersed, and they were allowed to remain.

Years later, one of their converts told them that he had been in the circle, and that they had every intention of burning the missionaries to death with their house. However, as they approached the dwelling, there stood before the door a figure in white apparel holding a flaming sword. They fled in fright. And thus the door was opened for the Gospel in Tibet, because God honored the faith of those who were willing to die at any time for their Lord.

Although many of the first-century apostles died a martyr's death, Paul did not intimate that all would. We must take into account the adverb *hoos* in our text; the Lord has proven us "as if" we were sentenced to die at any time. He has proved our readiness to die for Him, Paul says. It is our attitude toward life and death that the Lord wants to prove worthy of Him who gave His life as a ransom for us, when He could have saved it.

However, as servants of Christ we are not to precipitate danger or invite unnecessary persecution. We should not bring ourselves to the brink of death, but should be ready for such a situation if and when the Lord decided to bring it about. Let us not tempt God by irresponsible behavior, because self-incurred martyrdom does not bring the glory to God that He desires.

> I would be yielded to Jesus,
>   Bearing His banner on high,
> Ready to live for His glory,
>   Equally ready to die!
>
> I would be yielded to Jesus—
>   Completely forever, His own!
> Living my life for His glory,
>   Yielded to Jesus alone.
>
> —Connie Calenburg

How Does Your Life Square with Your Profession of Faith?

In the last two sections, we have seen how the disciples of the Lord Jesus were made willing to accept a lowly place in life, and even to face death itself if necessary, for God's glory. It's interesting to note how the disciples and apostles are said to have found their death.

Matthew suffered martyrdom by being slain with a sword at a distant city of Ethiopia.

Mark expired at Alexandria, after being cruelly dragged through the streets of that city.

Luke was hanged upon an olive tree in Greece.

John was cast into a large kettle of boiling oil, but escaped death in a miraculous manner, and was afterward exiled to Patmos, where he died.

Peter was crucified head downward in Rome.

James the Greater was beheaded in Jerusalem.

James the Less was thrown from a lofty pinnacle of the Temple and then beaten to death with a blacksmith's club.

Bartholomew was flayed alive.

Andrew was bound to a cross from which he preached to his persecutors until he died.

Thomas was run through the body with a lance at Coromandel in the East Indies.

Jude was shot to death with arrows.

Matthias was first stoned and then beheaded.

Barnabas was stoned to death at Salonica.

Paul, after various tortures and persecutions, was at length beheaded at Rome by the Emperor Nero.

Such was the fate of these servants of Christ according to various traditional sources. As disciples and apostles their lives were constantly at stake. In certain sections of the world this is still true today of the missionaries of the cross. Death, physical death, may be around any corner. This is really not a detriment to anyone's life but a great blessing. To be ready to die at any moment, and to be sure that you are in the center of God's will, is cause for the greatest peace of heart anyone can enjoy in this life. You can live fully when you are ready to surrender life as if you had accomplished all God meant for you to do till then. What would you do if this were to be the last day of your life? That's the attitude you should have now. If God were to put you to the test, would He prove you willing to die for Him?

Paul was willing to be made a spectacle before

all. The word "spectacle" in the Authorized Version is actually "theater," *theatron* in Greek. The word is derived from the verb *theaomai,* which means to see or observe with our physical eyes. People go to the theater to watch other people engaged in some sort of drama. In the ancient world, everywhere you go you will find the ruins of a theater. It was actually a place of visual education and entertainment for the people.

When we say we are Christians, the world may not listen. But when we act like Christians, in all sincerity, of course, it becomes a living drama that commands attention.

Gustav Dore, the famous artist, once lost his passport while traveling in Europe. When he came to the boundary post between two countries and was asked for his passport, he fumbled about and finally announced, "I have lost it, but it is all right. I'm Dore, the artist. Please let me go in."

"Oh, no," said the officer. "We have plenty of people representing themselves as this or that great person! Here is a pencil and paper. Now, if you are Dore the artist, prove it by drawing me a picture."

Dore took the pencil and drew some pictures of scenes in the immediate area. "Now I am perfectly sure you are Dore. No one else could draw like that!" said the officer as he allowed Dore to enter the country.

So it is with us. People follow what we do on the stage of life. They look to see if our conduct squares with our profession. Are we drawing the picture of Christ, as it were, or of a different person? What the world wants to see is reality in our actions. It has been said that God has great and wonderful things to display if He finds suitable showcases. Are you a good showcase for Jesus Christ?

The world watches us, says Paul, just as people go to watch a theatrical performance. They follow our actions and our words. They evaluate us. They learn through what we do and what we say.

When Dr. Will H. Houghton was pastor of Calvary Baptist Church in New York City, a glib-tongued salesman came into his study and offered him some oil stocks that he said would make him a fortune. Dr. Houghton looked at the man and said in substance, "If this stock is as good as you say, why aren't you rich? You come in here in a shabby suit, with shoes run down at the heels, and expect me to believe you represent a going concern? I suggest you get into some line of work that produces representatives who inspire more confidence in their product."

By our actions, our love, our spirit of self-sacrifice, do we inspire confidence in the Lord whom we profess to serve, and whom we seek to lead others to accept as Saviour and Lord? In the lines of an oft-quoted poem, remember, "We are the only Bible the careless world will read. . . . What is the Gospel according to you?"

The Drama of Your Life

All the world's a stage," said Shakespeare, "and all the men and women merely players." But players presuppose an audience, and in writing to the Corinthian Christians Paul tells them that the audience watching the lives and actions of the apostles was both earthly and heavenly. "For we are made a spectacle . . . to angels, and to men."

The theater in ancient Corinth was large and open-roofed. Often there was a full house to see its variety entertainment. The officials came and so did the whole city. Paul is telling the Corinthians that God's theater is larger than that, and open-roofed

80

under the vault of heaven. The people who play in a theater are often quite famous. In our day we call them stars. Popularity and theater performances are almost synonymous. But the apostles were not leading the lives of popular theatrical stars. Their lives were not filled with pleasure; they were not rich or famous. They were last on the social and economic ladder.

And yet they performed with an audience larger than those who were swimming in pleasure, wealth, and fame. They had a vertical audience as well as a horizontal one. Angels from above watched them, and men from every walk of life.

To be admired is one of man's deepest desires. It is inherent in our Adamic nature. The people of the world and carnal or immature Christians actively seek admiration. The worst affront you can give such people is not to pay any attention to them. But deeply committed or mature Christians don't speak or act for the purpose of being admired, or of drawing attention to themselves. Nevertheless that is inescapable. Though they don't seek it, yet heaven and earth cannot ignore them. "We became a theater to the world," declares Paul, "both angels and men."

Observe the verb "we became." In the Authorized Version it reads "we are made." In Greek it is *egeneetheemen*, from the verb *ginomai*, meaning "to become." Since the verb is in the aorist tense, passive voice, it should be translated, especially in this context, "we were made to become." It indicates that the apostles were not putting on a show, but that God Himself caused them to be observed by angels and men.

A theatrical presentation is a pretense. It's acting the part of someone else. It's making oneself temporarily be what one is not. But that's not what sincere and dedicated Christians do. They don't pretend to be what they are not. The Christian plays a role in this world, but he acts out what Christ has transformed him to be, and not what he merely makes a pretense of being.

The apostles became a spectacle to the world. It was not an occasional show of Christianity they put on, but their whole life was made by God to become a show of the Christ-life to the world. And so should our lives be, if we are really spiritual Christians. We are not to put on a mere show of piety, but let our lives be a day-by-day enactment of our life in Christ.

The Christian has a larger audience than any theatrical star because the show is continuous and to a large extent unconscious. He does not play on the stage from time to time for the purpose of calling attention to himself, but his whole life is a show that is being observed whether he realizes it or not. The spectators are also far more illustrious—not only men, but also angels.

In Hebrews 12:1 the apostle speaks of our being "compassed about with so great a cloud of witnesses," and in I Peter 1:12 we read of "things the angels desire to look into." Why do angels follow our actions on the stage of life? They watch with wonder the endurance with which we perform our God-assigned roles. Acting is an arduous task. Many actors collapse from the effort involved, often right on stage. The angels watch to see whether we are able to endure to the end of life's drama. They also strengthen and minister to us. "Are they not all ministering spirits, sent forth to minister for them who shall be heirs of salvation?" (Heb. 1:14).

Angels do follow our activities and they rejoice over our fruitful witnessing. In Luke 15:10 the Lord Jesus says, "there is joy in the presence of the angels of God over one sinner that repenteth." In order for them to rejoice, they must necessarily observe what is going on. We may be confident that angels do observe us and enable us to endure.

St. Francis said one day to one of the young monks, "let us go down into the town and preach."

They passed through the streets and returned to the monastery without having said a word. "You have forgotten, father," said the young man, "that we went down to the town to preach."

"My son," Francis replied, "we have preached. We were preaching as we walked. We have been seen by many: our behavior has been noticed: it was thus that we preached. It is no use, my son, to walk anywhere to preach unless we preach everywhere as we walk."

Wherefore, seeing we are compassed about by so great a cloud of witnesses, let us play our part nobly, looking unto Jesus, the Author and Finisher of our faith.

Who's Watching You?

When I get to heaven, will I be an angel?" a little girl asked her Sunday school teacher. She was quite surprised when the teacher told her that this was a mistaken notion, and that the Bible did not teach this at all.

R. A. Torrey, in answer to the question, "Has every child a guardian angel?" quotes Matthew 18:10: "Take heed that ye despise not one of these little ones; for I say unto you, that in heaven their angels do always behold the face of my Father which is in heaven." He comments: "The angels of the children here spoken of are the angels who watch over the children. This seems to be the plain teaching of the text. Some explain the text in another way, that the angels of the children spoken of here are the departed spirits of the children in the glory, but there is not a hint in the Bible anywhere that the departed spirits of human beings are angels. The clearest distinction is kept all through the Bible between angels and men. The old hymn, 'I Want to Be an Angel,' has no warrant in Scripture."

Angels are spiritual creatures, created by God for the service of mankind. As John Calvin says, "The angels are the dispensers and administrators of the Divine beneficence toward us; they regard our safety, undertake our defense, direct our ways, and exercise a constant solicitude that no evil befall us."

In the Bible we have many instances of angels exercising these functions.

In the Book of Acts we read that Philip the evangelist was preaching in Samaria. Men followed what he was doing; but so did angels. One of the angels acted as God's messenger to him. "And the angel of the Lord spake unto Philip, saying, Arise, and go toward the south unto the way that goeth down from Jerusalem unto Gaza, which is desert" (Acts 8:26). The angel knew that Philip would meet an Ethiopian there to whom God wanted him to witness.

While John was on the island of Patmos, an exile for Christ's sake, angels ministered to him. It was there that the Lord revealed to John the unfolding panorama of the future, "by his angel" (Rev. 1:1).

In the 5th chapter of Daniel we find that an angel was following the ungodly actions of Belshazzar in Babylon. The king had invited a thousand of his followers to celebrate the greatness of his kingdom. They desecrated the sacred vessels they had taken from the Temple at Jerusalem. They worshiped before idols of wood and stone, silver and gold. The hand of an angel sent from God wrote on the palace wall, "Mene, mene, tekel, upharsin," which meant, "Your kingdom is finished. You have been weighed in the balances and found wanting" (see Dan. 5:25-27).

Later on, in Daniel 9:22, we read that it was an angel who informed him what was going to happen in the world ultimately.

In other instances we read of Jacob being ministered to by angels. It was an angel who announced the changing of his name to Israel at Peniel (Gen. 32:1, 24-30, Hosea 12:3-6).

Angels followed the lives of Moses and Abraham (Exod. 3, Num. 20:16). Isaiah, speaking of the children of Israel coming out of Egypt, says, "In all their affliction he was afflicted, and the angel of his presence saved them: in his love and in his pity he redeemed them; and he bare them, and carried them all the days of old" (Isa. 63:9).

In the New Testament, we read that it was an angel who appeared to Zacharias the priest and announced that his wife would bear him a son, John the Baptist. It was the same angel Gabriel who announced to the Virgin Mary that she was going to bring forth Jesus (Luke 1:35). And the same angel instructed Joseph to take Mary as his wife, in spite of the fact that she was already expecting a child as a result of the energy of the Holy Spirit in her life (Matt. 1:20).

We who love and serve the Lord are being followed by angels. They follow our performance on life's stage and assist us when we are in danger of faltering. Their assistance is worth more than the reliance the natural men and carnal Christians place on their accumulated pleasures, resources, and people over whom they exercise power.

You may be at the bottom of the social,

economic, and political ladder, Paul tells the Corinthians, but look who's watching your drama of endurance in the world—angels! That's more important than having all the armies of the world at your command. It's interesting to note that after the word "world" Paul mentions "angels" before "men." Angels are more important spectators for the Christian than men are.

The word for "world" in I Corinthians 4:9 is *kosmoo* (dative of *kosmos*), which refers to the created material universe. Paul doesn't use the word *aiooni*, "age," which would have implied time, but *kosmoo*, the material universe as we know it. In our present state of existence as an immaterial spirit-soul and a material body, we are followed and influenced by the created material world around us and above us. But the material *kosmos* as we know it is also being linked with purely spiritual forces and personalities such as those of the angels.

This is especially true of those of us who are basically "spiritual" in our born-again personalities. Who can deny that metaphysical forces influence and inspect us in our physical world?

Our Angel Guardians

If an angel from heaven suddenly became visible to you as you were sitting alone, what would your reaction be? An ancient saint admonished Christians in these words: "In every apartment . . . in every corner, pay a respect to your angel. Dare not do before him what you dare not do before others. Consider with how great respect, awe, and modesty we ought to behave in the sight of the angels, lest we offend their holy eyes, and render ourselves unfit for their company. Woe to us if they who could chase away our enemy be offended by our negligence, and deprive us of their visit."

We have a number of illustrations in Scripture that show angels observing the believers on earth and assisting them in times of need. The angels are the created but immaterial personalities of heaven who can take on temporary form and shape at will, so that they can at times actually be observed by the permanently material personalities of men who in their basic essence are spiritual beings. It is not a critical and chastening oversight that the angels exercise on behalf of dedicated apostles and lay Christians, but rather a helpful one.

One illustration concerns the life of the prophet Elisha. While he was at Dothan, the King of Syria sent his army against him. One of Elisha's assistants informed Elisha that the armies of the enemy had surrounded them. Elisha replied, "Fear not: for they that be with us are more than they that be with them" (II Kings 6:16). Elisha then prayed that his assistant might see the invisible armies on which Elisha was counting. "And the Lord opened the eyes of the young man; and he saw: and, behold, the mountain was full of horses and chariots of fire round about Elisha" (v. 17). This was the angelic host sent by God to encourage and protect Elisha.

We also find an interesting account of an angelic visitation to Paul recorded in Acts 27:23-25. And it may be that this event was vivid in his mind as he wrote to the Corinthians, "We became a theater to the world, both to angels and men." It seems that Paul was on his way to Rome in a ship carrying more than 200 persons. A great storm came up, and they were in danger of sinking. Paul sought to encourage the crew, for they were terrified. His words are significant, for they reveal the role played by angels in the lives of believers in times of danger. "For there stood by me this night the angel of God, whose I am, and whom I serve, saying, Fear not,

Paul; thou must be brought before Caesar: and, lo, God hath given thee all them that sail with thee" (vv. 23, 24).

And David in Psalm 91 says that God "shall give his angels charge over thee, to keep thee in all thy ways. They shall bear thee up in their hands, lest thou dash thy foot against a stone" (vv. 11, 12).

The story is told of a little boy who asked his mother if he could take his baby sister out to play. She had just begun to walk alone, and could not step over anything that lay in the way. His mother said, "Yes, if you'll be careful not to let her fall."

The man who tells the story says, "I found them at play, very happy, in the field. I said, 'You seem to be very happy, George. Is this your sister?'

" 'Yes, sir,' he replied.

" 'Can she walk alone?'

" 'Yes, sir, on smooth ground.'

" 'Then how did she walk over those big stones between here and the house?'

" 'Well, Mother told me to be careful she didn't fall, so I put my hands under her arms, and lifted her up when she came to a stone, so she wouldn't hit her foot against it.'

" 'That's right, George. You see now how to understand that text, "He shall give his angels charge over thee. . . . They shall bear thee up in their hands, lest thou dash thy foot against a stone." God charges His angels to lead and lift His people over difficulties, just as you have lifted little Anne over these stones. Do you understand it now?' "

As far as the Christian is concerned, he is better off being watched over and protected by angels than by mighty armies of men. "The angel of the Lord encampeth round about them that fear him, and delivereth them" (Ps. 34:7).

In Acts 12:1-11 we read how Herod the King

had imprisoned Peter with the intention of putting him to death. But God intervened. As Peter was sleeping, an angel appeared and awoke him. "Arise up quickly," said the angel. "And [Peter's] chains fell off from his hands" (Acts 12:7). And Peter, following the angel, was liberated from prison, past locked doors and unseeing guards.

This, of course, doesn't imply that God always sends His angels to deliver us in time of trouble. God knows what is best in the furtherance of His over-all plans. If it is His will in His eternal wisdom and providence to deliver us, nothing can stop Him or the angels He sends to accomplish it. Peter and Paul, who were delivered on many occasions, were finally delivered by the hand of God to a cruel enemy. This was not because God could protect them in some instances and not in others, but because He knows and chooses when it is time for our earthly performance to end.

Whose Favor Should
a Christian Seek,
Man's or God's?

"We are fools for Christ's sake, but ye are wise in Christ; we are weak, but ye are strong; ye are honourable, but we are despised" (I Cor. 4:10).

Wise Fools

No one wants to be thought a fool, a weakling, or beneath contempt. We all want to be considered wise and strong and worthwhile people. But a Christian is often placed in the position of having to choose between the favorable opinion of men or the approval of God. What a Christian, under the Spirit's guidance, chooses to be for Christ's sake may not be naturally pleasant, but if it is necessary then it can be greatly satisfying.

In I Corinthians 4:10 Paul presents three contrasts: foolishness versus wisdom, strength versus weakness, and honor versus disdain. He begins the verse with the personal pronoun "we." Who is meant by "we"? They are the apostles referred to in verse 9: "For I think that God hath set forth us the apostles last." He refers to himself and all others who have chosen to become Christ's disciples.

The word "apostles" here must not be taken in the strict and narrow sense of the Twelve Apostles in whose trust the Gospel was placed for faithful transmission. In its wider sense it means all those who are "blessed," *makarioi,* for Christ's sake, as our Lord so eloquently spoke of them in Matthew 5:1-10 and Luke 6:20-24. The important phrase in the Beatitudes is "for my sake" in Matthew 5:11, and "for the Son of man's sake" in Luke 6:22.

The word "blessed" refers to those indwelt by God, who are characterized by *makariotees,* "blessedness," a quality of Deity. The Lord said to His disciples, "Blessed are ye . . . for my sake," because of what I am and have done for you. When we are indwelt by God we are fully satisfied.

The Beatitudes teach us that, if it is necessary for us to confess our spiritual helplessness (poverty of spirit), to be sorrowful because of sin, to be meek (not taking offense at personal insults, but being angry only at sin), to show that we have no righteousness of our own, to be merciful and pure in heart, to be peacemakers, to be willing to be persecuted, reviled, and maligned, all for Christ's sake, we will not be any less satisfied, but rather more.

And then, in the Beatitudes in Luke, Christ pronounces those "blessed" who voluntarily accept poverty, hunger, tears, the hatred and rejection of worldly people, and being reproached and slandered for the sake of the Son of man. The Christian who is "blessed" is willing to undergo all these privations of life in a spirit of acceptance and even joy.

Worldly people may think a Christian who embraces poverty for the sake of Christ is "crazy" for not keeping what he is able to earn for himself, to be spent for his own pleasure. According to the judgment of the natural man, that person is "crazy"—a moron—who gives away so much of what he has that he himself must do without. Sacrifice is foolishness in the eyes of the world.

Paul, with all his natural ability and intelligence, could undoubtedly have been a successful businessman. But he chose to use his mind and enterprising ability for the Lord. As far as the world was concerned, he was a fool; but as far as God was concerned he was wise.

The decisions Christians make often seem foolish to the world. Why? Because the Christian seeks not his own material advantage or comfort but God's glory. When you put God in the center of your life, you are considered wise by those who have done the same thing. But selfish people will consider you foolish.

"We are fools [or morons, as the Greek text has it] for Christ" or "for Christ's sake." We must differentiate between the two expressions, "for Christ" (*dia Christon*) and "in Christ" (*en Christoo*). Notice that there are two prepositions used: "for," *dia,* and "in," *en.* We are considered fools for Christ's sake. Of course, we are not actually fools, but because our wisdom is different from the world's we are considered fools by the world, and we consider the worldly-minded who reject Christ for a life of sin and selfishness to be tragically foolish indeed. But we ourselves don't mind being considered fools as long as we have His approval, and know it is "for Christ's sake."

This reminds me of a street-corner evangelist who often went around wearing a sandwich board with the words, "I'm a fool for Christ's sake. Whose fool are you?"

The Wisdom of Men Vs. the Wisdom of God

Why are Christians often regarded as fools?

It's because they believe what seems foolish in the eyes of the world: God's Son born in a cattle stall; the Messiah working as a carpenter; the Saviour of the world crucified with criminals; the almighty God buried in a tomb; salvation without any deeds, merits, or virtue on our part; Christ dying for the ungodly; the pious, strict, right-living Pharisee condemned, and the wretched, sinful publican justified. "How unthinkable! How ridiculous!" cries the world. "Only a fool would believe in a religion like that!"

But Paul saw it with clearer vision: "The foolishness of God is wiser than men; and the weakness of God is stronger than men" (I Cor. 1:25). The very thing that seems foolish to men is in fact eternal wisdom; and the very plan that appears to men as wholly wrong has actually been worked out in the councils of God, and so is divinely right. The way of salvation devised by God is so unique, so far superior to anything conceived by the mind of man, that its apparent foolishness is in reality the most profound and unsearchable wisdom. If we are fools for believing that, we are "fools for Christ's sake!"

The difficult expression in this verse is "But you are [the verb is not there but understood] wise in Christ." Who is "you"? The quarreling and proud Christians alluded to in verses 6 and 7, who sought their satisfaction in the things of the world (v. 8). The danger is that consecrated Christians will consider such selfish and proud Christians as still in the world, as not having been born again by the Spirit of God. Paul wants to correct any such misapprehension by saying that they are "in Christ." There have always been selfish Christians in the local churches and in the Kingdom of God. Their selfishness ought not to lead to the hasty conclusion that they are unsaved. They are "in Christ" in spite of their natural abilities and achievements.

But the irony is that such selfish Christians consider themselves wise in their selfishness. And others of like mind applaud them as wise. Origen says that Paul was ironically advising the Corinthians to become wise in Christ. Yes, there are many believers who are "in Christ" but who are not disciples or learners in the sense that they are not wise toward God. With one hand they hold on to the Lord and with the other the world. They are fence-straddlers. Such half-hearted Christians can never enjoy Christ to the full extent that a whole-souled, unselfish Christian can.

Christian, since you are in Christ, don't seek to show off your worldly wisdom, either in the church or to your worldly associates. Preacher, ask yourself as you prepare your sermons, whether you are trying to show the wisdom that will commend you as wise in the eyes of the world, or the wisdom of God, which may lead the world to call you a fool.

In Corinth it was obvious that there were those who were preaching with an eye to acquiring a reputation for wisdom. It is quite possible that Apollos was one of that number. His background of Alexandrian philosophy was a great temptation. Paul had studied under Gamaliel, a prestigious accomplishment, but he was willing to be counted a fool for Christ. We preachers need to watch ourselves, lest we yield to the temptation of using our position to become celebrities, instead of exalting Christ as the Saviour of men. A man may become a famous preacher and not be a true disciple.

The first contrast of foolishness to wisdom here is more closely connected with teaching. But the second contrast concerns conduct: "We, weak, but ye, strong." The expressions "for Christ" and "in Christ" are understood in this antithesis also.

"We [are] weak for Christ [or for Christ's sake], but you [are] strong in Christ." What kind of weakness and strength is Paul referring to?

The Greek words are *astheneis* (plural), "weak," referring to people without strength, and *ischuroi* (plural), "strong." *Asthenees* (singular) is made up of the privative *a* "without," and the noun *sthenos,* "strength," meaning "without strength." *Ischuroi (ischuros,* singular) is a word used for "strong men," referring to leaders who have seized power into their own hands, such as dictators. Those who are in Christ do not seize political or social strength to the detriment of principle. It is rare indeed to find social or political strength being seized without some compromise of spiritual principles. Somehow earthly strength tends to dim our spiritual eyesight. If it comes to a choice between the two, which would you choose?

Undoubtedly Paul is referring here to social weakness and strength. The Christian who wants to live for Christ rarely wields much strength in society, in the economic, educational, and social strata of life. If any such strength comes to him, it is not because he sought it, but because it comes as a result of God's intervention and bestowal. It is not that a Christian is unable to ascend the ladder of influence, but that, as a true disciple of Christ, he will not do it at the cost of compromise with worldly standards of behavior.

The Temptation of Compromise

After Christ's baptism, you remember that He was hurried into the wilderness to be tempted of the devil. And what was the nature of that temptation? It was the same kind that comes to us when somebody says of us, when we are proposing some high course of action, "Don't be a fool."

We read that the first thing Satan said to our Lord was, "If thou be the Son of God, command that these stones be made bread" (Matt. 4:3). In effect he was saying, "That's what the people like; give them that. There's no need for you to go by the way of Calvary. The world respects strength, not weakness. Let them see your miracles. They love miracles. They're a sign of power. Go ahead. Don't be a fool."

But Jesus' response was, "In My view of man, there are things that a man eventually recognizes his need for more than food." Let's imagine the rest of what might have taken place. "Oh, well," said the devil, "if You take that line, let's go up to the top of the temple. Now," he said, "those people down there are all praying for the Messiah to come from heaven. That's what they're there for. Providential, isn't it? Jump down into the midst of them. If You are what You say You are, You won't be hurt. And they will acclaim You as the Messiah descended before their eyes from heaven, and the whole thing will be done. They love that kind of thing."

Yes, Christ was tempted to usurp power at the cost of compromise with principle, just as we are. But He left us an example, "that ye should follow his steps" (I Pet. 2:21). He chose the seemingly foolish way of the cross to conquer the hearts of men, rather than the way of worldly might and ostentatious miracle.

A Christian who is a faithful disciple often looks weak to the world. They cannot understand someone who loves his enemies instead of hating them; who blesses those who persecute him; who prays for those who are spiteful toward him, and turns the other cheek to those who slap him. They cannot appreciate the strength of character in a man who forgives those who wrong him; who denies himself and says "no" to the things that are tempting to the flesh; who travels the strait and narrow path, and who, if necessary, is ready to forsake father and mother for Christ's sake. They suspect the sanity of a man who serves his neighbor and regards him more highly than himself; who renounces his pride and ambition for Christ's sake, and places no trust in himself, his own merits and works.

"What a foolish way of life!" men say. "But God hath chosen the foolish things of the world to confound the wise; and God hath chosen the weak things of the world to confound the things which are mighty . . . that no flesh should glory in his presence" (I Cor. 1:27, 29).

(See "The Fool," in *The Chapel Hour*, by T. Coates, pp. 51-53.)

The third contrast presented by Paul is "Ye are honourable" in Christ, "but we are despised" for Christ's sake. Observe that the order is changed here. The "you [are] honourable" comes before the "we [are] despised." That is the estimate of the world in regard to how Christians live. The non-dedicated ones are accepted and esteemed; the dedicated ones are held in contempt for renouncing the world's values.

The word "honourable" here is *endoxoi*, "held in honor." It comes from the preposition *en*, "in," and the noun *doxa*, which means "high repute or recognition," and consequently "glory," which means recognizing a person for who and what he is. The tragedy is that some Christians do not consider being "in Christ" sufficient honor for them, but they seek the honor of men, and in the process often dishonor Christ. There is no greater honor and glory for men and women than to be in Christ. To be recognized by God is far more important than to be recognized by the world.

The word "despised" in Greek is *atimoi,* which is made up of the privative *a,* "without," and the noun *timee,* which primarily means "value or honor." We are without value, in the opinion of the world, because we have sold out to Christ. At best they treat us with condescension; at worst with disdain. We would be fully acceptable to them only if we compromised our position in Christ.

Again let us recall Christ's example. After Satan realized that Jesus could not be tempted to show His strength prematurely, he tried the "honor" bid—to achieve glory among men. He took Jesus to an exceedingly high mountain and showed Him all the kingdoms of the world. "Young man," he said in effect, "don't be a fool. Don't throw Your life away. Take my word for it, men are not worth the sacrifice You are proposing to make for them. They know what they want, and it's not what You have in mind to give them at all. Lower Your terms and You can have them now. Play up to them—or rather, play down to them—and You can have the whole thing." Think of it—the kingdoms of the world in a moment of time! "All this power will I give thee, and the glory of them" (Luke 4:6).

That was Satan tempting Christ, and that's how Satan tempts those who are in Christ—to seek the honor and glory of Satan and the world, instead of honor through sacrifice. We can only resist that temptation as Christ did, by rebuking Satan with the Word of God and the standard He sets for our lives.

Was Christ a Fool?

When Jesus Christ resisted the temptations of Satan in the wilderness, His final word to him was, "Get thee behind me, Satan: for it is written, Thou shalt worship the Lord thy God, and him only shalt thou serve" (Luke 4:8). The devil must have gone away muttering under his breath, "Fool, fool! His life won't be worth a snap of the fingers! He's going to throw it away when He doesn't have to."

Has Satan ever tempted you like that, telling you to seek the honor of men, to use your time and talents and energy for your own glory and enrichment, instead of for the glory of God, in accordance with His standards of righteousness?

Our Lord's own friends thought He was a fool. That must have been a hard thing to bear. His own mother, His relatives, thought He was beside Himself. The disciples thought He was foolish. When Jesus said He was going into Bethany, where people had tried to stone Him, His disciples, especially Peter and John, remonstrated with Him and asked Him why He proposed to do such a dangerous thing. He simply answered that He must, without giving any reason. There is no man who appears to the world so foolish as the kind of man who is under the compulsion of God's leading, and cannot give a reason. (See John 11:7-16.)

Judas particularly thought our Lord a fool for not asserting His power over His enemies. Some folk hold to the theory that Judas was not as bad as he's pictured. They claim he thought Jesus was foolish not to seize power when it seemed the time was ripe, and that Judas' idea in betraying Jesus was to force His hand. They say that Judas believed Jesus had some mysterious resource to call upon in an emergency, and could not really be taken by the enemy.

But if this viewpoint is valid, then Judas failed to understand our Lord. He planned to betray Him, believing that in the moment when the Roman soldiers were about to lay hands on Him Jesus would assert Himself and call down the heavenly forces to destroy His enemies, and then set up His Kingdom in the world. The night came, and the hour came, and the moment came, and Judas betrayed our Lord with a kiss. And the soldiers laid hands on Him, and He allowed Himself to be led away. At that moment Judas was sure He was a fool.

Pilate thought Jesus was a fool. He, like other Roman procurators, was scared to death that the Jews would revolt and his authority be lost. Actually we should not think of Jesus as standing before Pilate, but of Pilate standing before Jesus. In effect Pilate was asking Jesus, "What are you out for? What's your idea? What are you trying to accomplish?" And Jesus told him, "I am come to be a martyr to the truth." That's how the Greek reads. A martyr was basically a witness, according to the meaning of the Greek word. Cynically Pilate asked, "What is truth?" It was as though he had said, "My dear young man, take it from me, human beings are not worth the kind of thing You are proposing. You are offering pearls to swine, but they don't want pearls. They will let You down. They will let You die. They will forget all about You. I know them. Don't be foolish. You are young, only thirty-three. Don't throw Your life away for a dream."

But was Christ a fool? He knew that it was only by the seeming foolishness of the cross that men could be saved. Wisdom—divine wisdom—led Him to Calvary. His was not a wasted life but a sacrificed life, for the redemption of mankind.

The life you give to Christ is not thrown away, wasted, lost. It is a life buried with Him and then raised again in glory, even as His was. "Whosoever shall lose his life for my sake and the gospel's, the same shall save it" (Mark 8:36).

(See "Fools for Christ's Sake," by John A. Hutton, in *The Christian World Pulpit,* vol. 105, pp. 85-7.)

An unknown author penned these revealing words:

Jesus and Alexander died at thirty-three;
One lived and died for self; One died for you
and me.
The one died on a throne; the other on a
cross;
One's life a triumph seemed; the other but a
loss.
One led vast armies forth; the other walked
alone;
One shed a whole world's blood; the other
gave His own.
One won the world in life and lost it all in
death.
The other lost His life to win the whole
world's faith.

Jesus and Alexander died at thirty-three;
One died in Babylon; and One on Calvary.
One gained all for self; and One Himself He
gave;
One conquered every throne; the other every
grave.

The one made himself God; The God made
Himself less;
The one lived but to blast; the other but to
bless!
When Alexander died, forever fell his throne
of swords;
But Jesus died to live forever Lord of lords.

Jesus and Alexander died at thirty-three;
The one made all men slaves; but Christ made
all men free.

One built a throne on blood; the other built on
     love;
The one was born of earth; the other from
     above.
One won all this earth, to lose all earth and
     heaven.
The other gave up all, that all to Him be given.
The one forever died; but Christ forever lives;
He loses all who gets, and wins all things who
     gives.

Adapted

The Joy of Sacrificing for Christ

"Even unto this present hour we both hunger, and thirst, and are naked, and are buffeted, and have no certain dwellingplace" (I Cor. 4:11).

No Exemptions for Christians

One of the ministries that has been my chief joy for many years has been inserting Gospel messages as paid ads in newspapers and magazines all over the world. It has been more fruitful in reaching Hindus, Moslems, and other "unreachables" with the good news of salvation in Christ than any other form of evangelism.

But in order to effect this in most countries, it is first necessary to find a qualified man of God who is willing to suffer the consequences of promoting the Gospel so publicly. A man who is afraid to suffer for Christ will never be able to stand the pressures that will be brought upon him.

One of the most difficult non-Christian countries to reach is Muslim Pakistan. At a time when leaders from all over the Muslim world were gathered there to formulate plans to hinder the progress of the Christian faith, a Canadian missionary decided to stick his neck out and approach Muslim newspaper editors about publishing Gospel messages. He succeeded in getting them into one newspaper called *Imroze*. The first message drew 1,373 responses from Muslims who wanted to learn about Jesus Christ through the Gospel portion and Christian literature offered in the article.

This gave the missionary courage to take more audacious steps. In his letter he wrote: "I was in Lahore, which is about 250 miles from here. I visited the *Mashriq* newspaper office, a national newspaper here in Pakistan. *Mashriq* means 'East.' The men in the advertisement section of their big office were dumfounded when they realized that a man from such a land of opportunity as Canada had chosen to live in a 'backward' area of the world in order to preach the Gospel. It gave me a good opportunity to witness briefly and explain why I was willing to sacrifice and come to Pakistan happily for Christ's sake. They are all just dying to go to Canada.

"The great thing of the visit was that they agreed to take my ad for all the major cities where the *Mashriq* is published, namely, Lahore, Karachi, Peshawar, and Quetta. These cities cover the entire country of Pakistan, almost like the four corners. . . . The pile of mail still unanswered indicated that there could be a total of 2,000 requests for Christian literature from Muslims."

This is a good illustration of the attitude of the Apostle Paul intimated in I Corinthians 4:11. "Even unto this present hour we both hunger, and thirst, and are naked, and are buffeted, and have no certain dwellingplace." The phrase "for Christ," or "for Christ's sake" *(dia Christon)* in verse 10 has to be

106

understood as the motivation of the attitude of the Christian, and especially an apostle, to be willing to go without the physical necessities of life.

"Even unto the present hour." Why does Paul speak in this way? He closes verse 13 in a similar manner: "Being defamed, we intreat: we are made as the filth of the world, and are the offscouring of all things *unto this day.*" This is what he had found necessary to suffer for Christ's sake up to this point. But that did not mean it had to be like that forever. Paul could only look back over his experiences to see that his Christian life and ministry, to be what it was, had to include sacrifices for the sake of Christ.

The first lesson we learn from this verse is that life in Christ is not exempt from trouble, trial, and privation. Because we are Christians, we are not to suppose we are immune from the common distresses of life. Sickness and care, loss and pain, come to Christians as to others. In fact, sometimes it seems as if the godly had the larger share of life's misfortunes. David recognized this when he wrote, "Many are the afflictions of the righteous: but the Lord delivereth him out of them all" (Psalm 34:19).

We find an excellent illustration of this in the life of Elijah the prophet. God had used him to cause the drought to punish Ahab and the followers of Baal. But the Lord sent Elijah to the flowing waters of the brook Cherith. As he sat there enjoying God's special provision, he may have thought himself exempt from the common sufferings of humanity. But we read in I Kings 17:7, "And it came to pass after a while, that the brook dried up." Elijah was deprived, too. He suffered thirst. It was God's way of teaching him that even as God's prophet he was not exempt from the physical calamities of life. It was not punishment for disobeying God; it came in spite of his implicit and prompt obedience.

107

God is the Creator, possessor, preserver, and distributor of all things—physical and spiritual—but He does not necessarily enrich all believers materially. It's easy enough to say, "God's servant deserves the best." He may indeed deserve it, according to human estimate and expectation. But the fact of the matter is that our material abundance is not always proportionate to our commitment to Jesus Christ. In fact, it's often quite the opposite. If ever there was a person who was committed to Christ, it was Paul. And yet, as he looked back upon his entire life up to this point, he said, "Even unto this present hour we both hunger, and thirst, and are naked, and are buffeted, and have no certain dwelling-place." In other words, he says, in spite of his dedication to Christ he has not materially prospered.

The Formula for Happiness

Though the Apostle Paul spoke of his great privations endured for the sake of Christ, he knew that the situation could change in the future. He would have welcomed it if it had pleased God to change it. He was just as human as we are in liking to eat, satisfy our thirst, and have a comfortable house to live in. But since privation was the state God permitted him to be in for the sake of the Gospel, he did not complain.

Remember what he wrote to the Philippians? "Not that I speak in respect of want" for I have learned, in whatsoever state I am, therewith to be content." And then he added, "I know both how to be abased, and I know how to abound: every where and in all things I am instructed both to be full and to be hungry, both to abound and to suffer need" (Phil. 4:11, 12).

There we have the formula for happiness. Of course, we are not to idolize privation and force ourselves to embrace it if there is no need. Certain people think it a virtue to go hungry and thirsty and live like nomads, because they feel there is an intrinsic value in poverty. That's not the point at all. If, for the sake of Christ, we have to go without certain necessities in serving Him, as Paul did, we should do so without complaint. But let's not confuse the goal with the means. Christ should be exalted and glorified, not we by calling attention to our privations. We must ask ourselves, "Who is at the center of my privation—self or Christ? Is it to show off my humility, or to advance the Kingdom of Christ?" Others may be able to glorify Christ through their wealth put at His disposal, and still others by their poverty.

I believe that Paul indicated a chronological limit in describing his privations for Christ's sake because he knew that the future, especially when he laid down his mortal body, would be brighter than the present. "Until now . . . up to this hour . . . it has been physically rough," he seems to be saying, "but the future is as bright as the promises of God." Or as he puts it in Romans 8:18, 23, "For I reckon that the sufferings of this present time are not worthy to be compared with the glory that shall be revealed in us. . . . Even we ourselves groan within ourselves, waiting for the adoption, to wit, the redemption of our body."

This hope is what reduces the pangs of hunger, thirst, and exposure to the elements. If we are called upon to suffer for Christ's sake, let us do it with joy, knowing that a better day is coming.

Misjudged by a fellow missionary, David Livingstone gave up his house and garden at Mabotsa, with all the toil and money they had cost him, rather than have any scandal before the heathen. He began in a new place the labor of house and school building, and gathering the people around him. His colleague was so struck with his generosity that he said, had he known his intention, he never would have spoken a word against him. Parting with his garden cost Livingstone a great pang. "I like a garden," he wrote, "but Paradise will make amends for all our privations here." Paul says, "I endure all things for the elect's sakes, that they may also obtain the salvation which is in Christ Jesus" (II Tim. 2:10).

Paul mentions certain specific privations that he and other apostles had to suffer for the sake of Christ. These were physical necessities and constitute the highest degree of sacrifice. To give much out of our abundance, as the Corinthians were giving, as we deduce from II Corinthians 8:1-5, is not as great in the sight of God as to be willing as Paul was to go hungry, thirsty, be scantily clothed, beaten up, and homeless.

The translation of I Corinthians 4:11 leaves much to be desired. The Authorized Version begins the verse with "even"—"Even unto this present hour" we suffer all these things. But the word "even" does not apply at all to the phrase "unto this present hour," but to the verb *peinoomen*, "hunger." Actually it is the conjuction *kai*, meaning "and." In this usage it stands for emphasis and could be translated "even." The verse would then read, "To this present hour we even go hungry, we even go thirsty, we even go naked, we even are buffeted, we even have no dwelling place." Paul lists these privations as being the height of physical sacrifice. After all, what is more essential for our physical sustenance than food, water, clothing, protection from injury, and shelter? Without these we are exposed to death.

The poet, George Neumarck, knew that a right

attitude in the midst of trials could change suffering to blessing. He wrote:

> Leave God to order all thy ways,
>   And hope in Him, whate'er betide.
> Thou'lt find in Him, in evil days,
>   Thy all-sufficient strength and guide.
> Who trusts in God's unchanging love
> Builds on the rock that naught can move.
>
> Sing, pray, and swerve not from His ways,
>   But do thine own part faithfully;
> Trust His rich promises of grace,
>   So shall they be fulfilled in thee.
> God never yet forsook at need
> The soul that trusted Him indeed.

Going Hungry for Christ's Sake

The specific privation the Apostle Paul speaks of enduring in I Corinthians 4:11 is hunger. "We even are hungering, or go hungry." The Greek verb is *peinoomen,* present active indicative first person plural. This does not mean that Paul was actually without food when he was penning these words, but that his attitude was one of readiness to go hungry whenever necessary for the sake of Christ. He was not to seek such an occasion but to accept it joyfully when God saw fit to allow it. This particular use of the present tense indicates that Paul and other apostles at intervals actually did go hungry, and this was a repeated occurrence, though they were not always hungry, thirsty, or otherwise in want.

The same is true of thirst. "We even go thirsty." If the traveling that the apostles engaged in to make Christ known necessitated their going without food and water for a time, they were willing to accept it. The Lord was not against the satisfaction of physical hunger and thirst. You remember that Satan tempted our Lord when He was in a state of hunger after fasting in the wilderness forty days. "And when they were ended, he afterward hungered" (Luke 4:2). That was a natural result of our Lord's humanity. To desire food is no sin; it is God's gift, to be received with thankfulness.

However, Satan knew how strong a desire for food we all have, including the Lord Jesus. That's why he tempted Him to command the stones to become bread. Could He have done it? Of course He could. But He didn't always do what He could, but only what would serve the higher purpose for which He came into the world.

Can the Lord miraculously feed us when we have to go hungry for His sake? Of course He can. He did it on a number of occasions, as in the case of the Israelites and Elijah. But God is selective in the performance of His miracles. As far as Paul was concerned, he was willing to go hungry for Christ's sake at any time. He felt that God would be equally good if He chose to feed him miraculously—something we have no indication He ever did—or if He allowed him to feel the pangs of hunger to the degree that He saw fit. Our attitude should never be one of presuming to impose on God the results we would like to have.

Let's be careful not to misunderstand Paul and go hungry without a purpose because we think there's some merit in it. Think of that time when the Lord and His disciples were going through Samaria. The Lord sat on Jacob's well while His disciples went to buy food, for it was midday and they must have been hungry. The Lord didn't hinder their doing that which was natural for the sustenance of their bodies. Nor did He make food out of nothing, though He could have done it. But when they brought Him the food, He refused it. Why? Not because He wasn't hungry or didn't need it, but because He was satisfying a higher urge, to bring the Gospel to the Samaritan woman.

We, too, should be careful not to allow food to stand in the way of accomplishing the higher task of doing God's will. In this age, when we indulge in food so freely and thoughtlessly, each of us should pause to ask, "How much do my eating habits deprive me of opportunities to make Christ known?" Which comes first in our lives—Christ or the satisfaction of our creature comforts? "Master, eat. But he said unto them, I have meat to eat that ye know not of" (John 4:31, 32).

On one occasion Matthew invited his former colleagues to a meal at his house. Whom did he invite as the guest of honor? Jesus, the Master, Himself. Luke says he "made him a great feast in his own house: and there was a great company of publicans and of others that sat down with them" (Luke 5:29). The laxity of the new religious teacher in not adhering to Pharisaical laws of segregation moved the scribes and Pharisees to indignation. "How is it that he eateth and drinketh with publicans and sinners?" they asked in horrified surprise. (See Mark 2:16.)

When the Lord met Zacchaeus, He did not hesitate to go into his house, even though He knew that in such a well-to-do home He would be bountifully plied with food. Jesus ate food as matter-of-factly as anyone to sustain His body. His enemies accused Him of being a glutton and a winebibber. "The Son of man came eating and drinking, and they say, Behold a man gluttonous and a winebibber, a friend of publicans and sinners" (Matt. 11:19, Luke 7:34).

Of course, their accusations were malicious

and unjust. "A gluttonous man and a winebibber" is hardly consistent with Jesus' forty days' fast in the wilderness, or the statement that on one occasion He and His disciples "had no leisure so much as to eat" (Mark 6:31). And you remember His gentle rebuke to Martha for preparing too elaborate a meal (Luke 10:40-42).

We are quite sure Jesus was not "a gluttonous man and a winebibber." It does not harmonize with all we know of His character, with the supreme place that He accorded to the things of the Spirit. There was, however, a modicum of truth on which they based their charge, which might give it a superficial justification. Jesus did not make a great virtue of abstinence.

Willingness to Suffer for Christ

The Lord Jesus Christ did not regard fasting as an essential part of religion. In this He differed from the Pharisees, who fasted twice in the week as a religious duty (Luke 18:12). Neither did He resemble His forerunner, John the Baptist, who confined himself to such desert fare as locusts and wild honey (Mark 1:6). Jesus entered the homes of the people and accepted their hospitality without asking whether all the cooking and culinary operations had been carried out according to the strict rules of ceremonial cleanness. He was pleased to be the guest of Peter, Matthew, Zacchaeus, Martha and Mary, Simon the leper, and many others; and He doubtless paid His hosts and hostesses the compliment of enjoying the food set before Him. But when He deemed it necessary for a higher purpose to go without food, He did not hesitate. Such was Paul's attitude. Such should be ours.

The other verb in I Corinthians 4:11, "We even go thirsty," has the same meaning. Whenever

Paul felt it necessary to sacrifice water for the sake of Christ, he gladly did so. Observe, however, that Paul uses the first person plural. He makes sure to include many other dedicated apostles and servants of Christ. He does not want to give the impression that he alone is willing to sacrifice by going hungry and thirsty.

Each of these experiences Paul describes was also the experience of our Lord on earth. He hungered and thirsted. On the cross He said, "I thirst" (John 19:28). He did not have to go to the cross or suffer thirst; He did it for our sakes. Thirst is a dreadful feeling, as it grows accumulatively worse. And for Him to cry out an agonizing "I thirst!" it must have been unbearable. How many times have we willingly suffered for Christ's sake, because of what He did for us?

In his enumeration of the necessities of life that we as Christians—and particularly as ministers of the mysteries of God—should be willing to forego if necessary for Christ's sake, he mentions food, water, and then clothing. "Even we shiver in the cold." The Greek verb is *gumniteuomen,* which comes from *gumnos,* meaning "naked, stripped, bare." It also means being without an outer garment, something no decent person would go without in public. It signifies being poorly dressed. Again, that doesn't mean we as Christians should go about shabbily or inadequately dressed. But we should be willing to spend less on clothes, or even graciously accept "hand-me-downs," for the sake of Christ.

The principle here is not to consider giving up luxuries a sacrifice, but giving up such essentials as food, drink, and clothing. We can be just as nicely and warmly dressed for less money, and have more money for the proclamation of the Gospel. Again the question to ask is, "How wasteful am I in the matter of clothing? Am I dressing to show off?"

Paul may be referring to a willingness to give some of his clothing to others. I've been on both ends of this experience—the receiving and the giving. I remember when I first came to the United States from a warm climate. It was cold and I had no overcoat. How grateful I was to that servant of Christ, Melvin Wampler, who took off his coat and placed it on my shoulders. He went without so that I could be warm. In a similar manner I have often endeavored to do this for others. Believe me, however, there is more joy in giving and going without than in receiving and possessing.

A young man named John saw some ragged boys and invited them to Sunday school. One boy said he would go, but he had no coat. John gave him his coat and went in with him. Years afterward, a teacher of a Bible class told the story. A man in his class said, "I was that boy, and Dr. John G. Patton, one of the most famous missionaries of the ages, gave me his coat." Sometimes a servant of Christ is called upon to keep others warm by being cold himself.

The next verb in I Corinthians 4:11 is "we are buffeted." In Greek it is *kolaphizometha,* which literally means "to be struck with the fist." This is what they did to our Lord when He was tried by the high priests. The same word is used in Matthew 26:67: "Then did they spit in his face, and buffeted him," or "beat him with their fists," as the New American Standard Version correctly renders it. If our Lord was roughly treated and beaten with men's fists, let's ask ourselves, "Would I be willing to undergo rough treatment for His sake?" Or are we going to deny Him in order to avoid being roughly treated, even as Peter denied Him in the hour of His

116

trial? Paul was willing to be struck with the fist, to be roughly treated, for Christ's sake. Are we?

It is a memorable tribute that is paid to the martyrs in the Epistle to the Hebrews (11:35): "Others were tortured, not accepting deliverance." Too often we are tempted to accept deliverance, any kind of deliverance, on any pretext, as long as it excuses us from suffering. How much more Christlike it is to pray for grace to "endure unto the end."

As Paul said to those Christians who attempted to dissuade him from going to Jerusalem, "What mean ye to weep and to break mine heart? for I am ready not to be bound only, but also to die at Jerusalem for the name of the Lord Jesus" (Acts 21:13).

Facing Life's Trials with Courage

The last trial of which Paul speaks in I Corinthians 4:11 is expressed by the Greek verb *astatoumen,* "Even we have no certain dwelling-place." This verb comes from *astateoo,* which means "to be unsettled, homeless, not to have a permanent place to live." Paul certainly knew by experience what this meant. He constantly traveled from place to place, with no permanent place to call home.

In this he was like his Lord, who said, "Foxes have holes, and birds of the air have nests; but the Son of man hath not where to lay his head" (Luke 9:58, Matt. 8:20). What was Jesus' permanent address on earth as He ministered to the multitudes? We know He lived in Capernaum, but He had no house of His own. He was a guest in various homes. He who created all things did not select one to make His own special dwelling place. What was Paul's permanent address? No one knows. He was constantly traveling to make Christ known.

117

How different we are, in our desire to put down roots and achieve a sense of security. When we find a place we like we say, "This is it. I'm not going to move from this place until they carry me out feet first. This is my home, and I intend to stay here for good." Maybe for your own good, but what about the Lord's and His Kingdom?

"Too bad, son, that you don't have a home," said a sympathetic bystander to a little boy whose house had just burned to the ground. "Oh, but you're wrong, Mister," said the boy. "We have a home; we just don't have a house to put it in."

We may be sure of this: the servant of Christ may not have a permanent house, but he has a home no matter where he goes for the sake of Christ.

Let's ask ourselves this question: "Am I ashamed at what sacrifices I may be called upon to make in serving Christ?" Two young men were talking about this very thing. One of them said, "I cannot tell you all that the Lord Jesus is to me, or what He has done for me. I do wish you would enlist in His army." "I'm thinking about it," answered the other young man, "but it means giving up several things—in fact, I am counting the cost."

A Christian officer, just passing, heard the last remark, and laying his hand on the shoulder of the young soldier said, "Young man, you talk of counting the cost of following Christ, but have you ever counted the cost of not following Him?"

Paul was not in any way complaining as he enumerated his privations endured for Christ's sake. He considered them inevitable and actually rejoiced in them. Robert Hall, the great Baptist preacher, used to be subject to occasions of great physical pain in the course of which he would roll on the ground in sheer agony. But when the pain was over, the first words he used to say were, "I hope I didn't complain." How much more effective our witness for Christ would be if we didn't complain so much about our trials of faith.

Paul writes: "For Christ's sake up to this hour, we even go hungry, we even go thirsty, we are even dressed scantily, we are even treated roughly, we even have no permanent house to live in." But no word of complaint escaped his lips. He had learned to rejoice in tribulation. He sang his hymns of praise even at midnight when he lay in the inner dungeon at Philippi with his feet fast in the stocks. That was rough treatment. People couldn't help feeling there was something in the faith this man preached when they saw how it sustained him in the sea of troubles that surged over him.

Paul preached the Gospel of the love of God. The good news he had to proclaim was that God loved men so well that He gave His only Son to die for them. Well, at any rate, Paul's own conduct confirmed the Gospel he preached. For when it was blackest night with him he could sing, because he was so sure of the love of God. He commended himself as a true minister of God by the gallantry and joyful courage with which he faced life's trials and difficulties and calamities. How we face up to the inevitable difficulties and hardships which life brings is a pretty accurate test of the reality of our faith in God.

Chrysostom, the ancient Church Father, was a beautiful example of true Christian courage. When he stood before the Roman Emperor, he was threatened with banishment if he still remained a Christian. Chrysostom replied, "Thou canst not, for the world is my Father's house; thou canst not banish me."

"But I will slay thee," said the Emperor. "Nay, but thou canst not," said the noble champion

119

of the faith again, "for my life is hid with Christ in God."

"I will take away thy treasures." "Nay, but thou canst not," was the retort; "for, in the first place, I have none that thou knowest of. My treasure is in heaven, and my heart is there."

"But I will drive thee away from man, and thou shalt have no friend left." "Nay, and that thou canst not," once more said the faithful witness; "for I have a Friend in heaven, from whom thou canst not separate me. I defy thee; there is nothing thou canst do to hurt me."

Should a Preacher Work with His Hands? How Should We Face Reviling and Persecution?

"And labour, working with our own hands: being reviled, we bless; being persecuted, we suffer it" (I Cor. 4:12).

Manual Labor No Disgrace

King Antigonus, when he had not seen Cleanthes, the philosopher, for a long time, said to him, "Do you continue to grind (referring to the occupation by which he supported himself)?" "Yes, sir," replied the philosopher, "I still grind; and that I do to gain my living, and not to depart from philosophy."

Preaching is spiritual work, but no preacher should consider it beneath his dignity to engage in manual labor when necessary. Jesus Himself worked as a carpenter in Nazareth (Mark 6:3). To work with one's hands has the respect of most people. Paul didn't want people to get the idea that a preacher was an idler. Perhaps those whom he tried to win to Christ were of the opinion that to preach and pray were a lazy man's lot. That's why he chose

121

to work with his own hands, despite the fact that all his life he had been a literary man.

When young, he was sent by his parents to Jerusalem to escape the heathen influence of Tarsus. In Jerusalem he may have had a sister, as reference is made in Acts 23:16 to a nephew. At any rate, while there he studied "at the feet of Gamaliel," although Tarsus, his home city, was superior at that time in literary pursuits to Athens and Alexandria. It was the birthplace of many Stoic philosophies.

I believe it unlikely that Paul made his living by manual labor before his conversion. His parents must have been well off to be able to send him to Jerusalem to further his studies and become more involved in Judaic teaching. Yet we find Paul with a hand trade as an apostle. Did he learn it after he became a Christian, so that no one could accuse him of making preaching a gainful affair? It would seem so.

"We even labour, working with our own hands." The Greek verb translated "labor" is *kopioomen* (first person plural, active of *kopiaoo*), which means "to work hard, to become weary, tired, to toil." Although as an educated Jew he had not dirtied his hands with manual labor, he was not too proud to engage in it after he became a Christian. He repeatedly defends his philosophy of a working ministry.

In I Corinthians 9:1-15 he defends his right to have a wife, as the apostle Peter had, as well as his right of support from those to whom he ministered. Apparently Paul was a widower, since to be a member of the Sanhedrin he had to be married. He probably preferred to remain unmarried after his wife's death, so that he could have greater freedom to travel, preach, and establish churches. This was not because of a necessity laid upon him but by his own free choice.

The same was true with regard to his support. "Even so hath the Lord ordaincd that they which preach the gospel should live of the gospel" (I Cor. 9:14). But he preferred to be self-supporting, so that no one could accuse him of preaching for the sake of money and an easy life.

No doubt some people looked upon his manual labor as demeaning to his office, but in his case at least he believed it was the proper thing to do for Christ's sake. In II Corinthians 11:7 he writes: "Have I committed an offense in abasing myself that ye might be exalted, because I have preached to you the gospel of God freely (that is, without price)?" He didn't do it because the Corinthians were poor and unable to support a minister, but because he didn't want to bring offense on the Gospel (see II Cor. 8:1-5). He forfeited an available right in order to promote the glory of Christ. If there were more Pauls in the Christian ministry, more of the world would have been exposed to the Gospel. Paul gave up his right to be paid, not because there was no money in the treasury—for there was plenty—but because the reputation of Christ to the world and Paul's fellow believers was his overriding consideration.

How beautifully he reminds the Thessalonians of his conduct among them: "For ye remember, brethren, our labour (*kopon,* the noun form of the same word as in I Cor. 4:12) and travail: for labouring night and day, because we would not be chargeable unto any of you, we preached unto you the gospel of God" (I Thess. 2:9). And then again in II Thessalonians 3:8 he wrote: "Neither did we eat any man's bread for nought; but wrought with labour (*kopoo,* again the same word) and travail night and day, that we might not be chargeable to any of you." It was never because it was not right for a minister to be paid, but because he was willing to forfeit his rights for the sake of bearing a better testimony for Christ.

You Can Be a "Working Missionary"

When the Apostle Paul went to Corinth to preach the Gospel, he stayed in the home of Aquila, a tentmaker, and engaged in the same trade.

Had Paul expected to be paid everywhere he went to preach, it is doubtful whether he could have established any churches. We would not have had the Epistles to the Corinthians, or to the Ephesians, or to the Thessalonians, or any others from his pen. How could he ask for pay, since he was the pioneering missionary? When he came to Corinth, was he sent there by a supporting church—the believers he had led to Christ in Philippi, Berea, Thessalonica, or Athens? No, he went as a tentmaker and used that trade to support himself, as we see in Acts 18:3: "And because he was of the same craft, he abode with them (that is, Priscilla and Aquila), and wrought: for by their occupation they were tentmakers."

Someone reading these lines may be a businessman, as Aquila was in Corinth. Maybe there is no testimony for Christ in your area. Maybe you do not have a talent for teaching and preaching. Did you ever think of employing another Christian who can witness effectively for Christ? You will be served in your business and you will be used of God to provide another Paul-preacher-tentmaker for your spiritually needy community.

Or you may be a preacher who has some trade or profession in addition to being a preacher. If so, don't sit around waiting for some missionary society to send you out, or some church to call you. God has given you two hands with which to earn your living. The goal of a Christian's life should be to make Christ known. Making a living is only the means to the end. Why not discover where there is a need for Christian witness and seek employment there? Thousands of positions are open all over the world for Christians trained in the professions, trades, or services. Don't let them be filled by unbelievers where your testimony is so desperately needed. Would to God that every Biblically trained person also had the ability to work at a job to earn his living. Don't seek the jobs that pay most, but the jobs that will take you where your witness for Christ will count the most. That was Paul's philosophy; let it be yours also, and you can help bring about a spiritual revolution in the place God sends you.

Just the other day I received a letter from a man whose company offered him an opening in Malaysia. It's very difficult for a professional missionary to gain admission there. This Christian businessman accepted the offer—which meant living in a strange land without many of the usual comforts. But his presence there has meant the opening of a Christian church in his home. We need missionaries like that, in addition to those who are dedicating all their time to the Lord's work.

And a word to those of you who are professional missionaries: If the Lord lays a burden on your heart for an unreached area, consider getting the training for a needed job and going there as a working man with a missionary's heart. Sometimes, as I have observed missionaries in many parts of the world, I have felt that, had they been also working with their hands as Paul was in Corinth, the effectiveness of the Gospel outreach would be greater. Paul was a wise man to realize that such a course made the Gospel more acceptable to the people of Corinth and Thessalonica. Let's examine our hearts and attitudes before we conclude that we have no opportunities or results because the Lord is not blessing us. Are we fulfilling God's conditions of blessing?

As a servant of Christ, never feel that it is degrading to labor with your own hands as Paul did. The Lord of glory Himself came down to earth and labored in a carpenter's shop. And "the servant is not greater than his Lord" (John 13:16).

When Bishop Patterson went among the South Sea Islanders, the natives were surprised to see that he was ready to put his hand to anything. He would do a piece of carpentry, wash up things after meals, and teach the little ones to wash and dress themselves. Other people who came to the islands tried to push all the manual labor on to the natives. So to express the difference, they called the bishop a "gentleman-gentleman," and the others "pig-gentlemen."

Jesus Christ when on earth was called "the Carpenter"; and if one of His chief apostles, Paul, worked with his hands as a tentmaker, manual labor ought never to be thought beneath the dignity of a Christian minister.

On a Friday morning an eager young man from Stanford University stood before Louis Janin seeking part-time employment. "All I need right now," said Janin, "is a typist." "I'll take the job," said the young man, "but I can't come back until next Tuesday." On Tuesday he reported for duty. "Why couldn't you come back before today?" Janin wanted to know. "Because I had to rent a typewriter and learn to use it," was the unexpected answer. That quickly prepared typist was Herbert Hoover.

Do you know of a place where there is almost

no witness for Christ at all? Learn the job that will take you there. That's being as wise as Paul.

The only place in Scripture that gives us any indication Paul was a tentmaker is Acts 18:3. Priscilla and Aquila were tentmakers, and this verse says Paul "was of the same craft." When did Paul learn this trade? We don't know. Perhaps he learned it before going to Corinth, so he could find employment with Aquila. That's not really a farfetched assumption. You can do the same, with the exception that your employer need not be a Christian, as Priscilla and Aquila were. Your own hands, and the skill you acquire in using them, may help to fulfill your heart's desire to serve Christ where your life will count the most for Him.

When Is It Right to Speak Out?

The Greeks among whom the Apostle Paul lived and ministered in Corinth and Thessalonica called the mechanics *banausous,* "vulgars." They applied this epithet to those handicraftsmen and artisans who led a sedentary life. Such people were despised among warlike and nomadic people. They considered Paul's manual labor *banausos*—not hard enough. In modern parlance he was a "softy" in the eyes of these critical Greeks.

It is quite possible that this is one reason why Paul was reviled. Observe that "being reviled, we bless" comes immediately after his statement, "We even labor, working with our own hands." But tentmaking was considered a *banausos technee,* a vulgar trade, which might very well have given rise to Paul's reviling by the proud Greeks who could always find something for which to criticize him.

The Greek word translated "reviled" is *loidoroumenoi,* a common expression meaning "to reproach, to abuse verbally, to insult, to revile." In

127

public life in Greece, insult and calumny played a considerable part, whether among the heroes, in political life in the democracies, in comedy, or in the great orators. Not to be susceptible to such reviling was part of the art of living, though in fact a great deal of objective harm was done by this love of denigration. That's what Paul's enemies were trying to do by reviling him or remonstrating angrily with him.

In the New Testament we find the verb form of this word four times (John 9:28, Acts 23:4, I Cor. 4:12, I Pet. 2:23), the noun twice (I Tim. 5:14, I Pet. 3:9), and the adjective twice (I Cor. 5:11; 6:10).

To revile (*loidorein*, infinitive) is an un-Christian act in those guilty of it. *Loidoros*, "a reviler," is twice mentioned in lists of vices. In I Corinthians 5:11 Paul says, "But now I have written unto you not to keep company, if any man that is called a brother be a fornicator, or covetous, or an idolater, or a railer (*loidoros*), or a drunkard, or an extortioner; with such an one no not to eat." And in I Corinthians 6:10 he mentions among those who will not inherit the Kingdom of God, "nor thieves, nor revilers (*loidoroi*), nor extortioners."

In the Old Testament, reviling was especially forbidden against superiors. This is brought out in Acts 23:1-5, where Paul was brought before the Sanhedrin to answer his accusers. Ananias, the high priest, took exception to something Paul said and ordered those who stood next to Paul to smite him on the mouth. Filled with righteous indignation, and not knowing who Ananias was, Paul burst out, "God shall smite thee, thou whited wall: for sittest thou to judge me after the law, and commandest me to be smitten contrary to the law?" This was taken as reviling by those who stood by, because they said to Paul, "Revilest thou God's high priest?" Paul was immediately apologetic and said, "I wist not, brethren that he was the high priest: for it is written, Thou shalt not speak evil of the ruler of thy people."

Was Paul's action in this incident contrary to the claim he made in I Corinthians 4:12 that "being reviled, we bless"? Did he just give lip service to such a course of conduct, without carrying through on it in actual practice? Not really. His enemies were stretching a point when they called this reviling; Paul himself considered it righteous indignation. It was rather in the category of sinless anger. He himself in writing to the Ephesians said, "Be ye angry, and sin not" (Eph. 4:26).

The Lord Jesus acted and spoke in the same way under similar circumstances, as we see in Matthew 23. In fact, the whole tenor of His denunciations against the Pharisees could be taken as reviling, especially the words that are almost identical with those of Paul. Compare what the Lord called the Pharisees with what Paul called Ananias: "Woe unto you, scribes and Pharisees, hypocrites! for ye are like unto whited sepulchres" (Matt. 23:27). Paul's term for Ananias was "thou whited wall" (Acts 23:3). The characterization "whited" here actually means "whitewashed for the purpose of hiding your real self." It is an alternate expression for "hypocrite." But nobody dared call such language reviling when it was spoken by the Lord Jesus. They did not indulge in scathing words for the sake of rabble-rousing, but to rebuke those who were using the letter of the law to cloak their failure to keep the spirit of the law. In the name of religion they were oppressing those who were seeking to serve God in spirit and in truth. To keep silence would have been cowardice.

James Russell Lowell had nothing but scorn

for such people in the following lines:

> They are slaves who fear to speak
> For the fallen and the weak;
> They are slaves who will not choose
> Hatred, scoffing and abuse,
> Rather than in silence shrink
> From the truth they needs must think;
> They are slaves who dare not be
> In the right with two or three.

Our Lord spoke out in no uncertain terms against evil, regardless of the consequences; and the Apostle Paul followed closely in his Master's footsteps. Do we?

How to React to Our Enemies

In the New Testament there are several passages dealing with the way the Christian is to react when he is the object of reviling (*loidorein*) by others. In I Timothy 5:14 Paul advises, "Give none occasion to the adversary to speak reproachfully (*loidorein*)." This means that the Christian must avoid all occasion for calumny (*loidoria*).

The Lord warned believers that because of their association with Him they were subject to reproach. "Blessed are ye, when men shall revile (*oneidisoosin*, used here as a synonym) you" (Matt. 5:11). In the case of the blind man whom Jesus healed, as recorded in John 9:28, we read, "Then they reviled him (*eloidoreesan*), and said, Thou art his (Jesus') disciple; but we are Moses' disciples." Actually this was meant as a slur against Jesus.

We as Christians are to follow the example of our Lord, as recorded in I Peter 2:23, "Who, when he was reviled, reviled not again." Consider Him on the cross. When the scornful bystanders tried to make Him answer their reproach, He kept silence, as He had also done before Pilate. (See Matt. 26:63;

130

27:29, 44, John 18:23.) Note particularly the similarity of John 18:22, 23 to Paul's experience before the Sanhedrin. The Lord was smitten. "One of the officers which stood by struck Jesus with the palm of his hand, saying, Answerest thou the high priest so? Jesus answered him, If I have spoken evil, bear witness of the evil: but if well, why smitest thou me?" Here we see that the Lord Jesus objected to being smitten, even as Paul did. The Lord is not completely silent when reviled, but here He stresses the fact that His words were not wrongly spoken.

The principle that Christians are to follow is that they are not to revile those who revile them. As I Peter 3:9 says, "Do not repay evil with evil, or insult (*loidorian*) with insult (*anti loidorias,* reviling against reviling), but with blessing, because to this you were called, so that you may inherit a blessing." But the Christian, as shown by the example of the Lord Jesus and the Apostle Paul, need not remain wholly silent when he suffers abuse. He blesses not only by silence, but on occasion by indignant speech.

(See discussion in the *Theological Dictionary of the New Testament* by Gerhard Kittel, vol. IV, pp. 293-4.)

What does Paul mean by the expression "we bless," which he presents as the Christian reaction to the world's reviling? In Greek the word is *eulogoumen,* which can be transliterated "eulogize" or "speak well of." It comes from *eu,* "well," and *legoo,* "speak." Paul does not use the word *makarizomen,* from which the adjective *makarios,* "blessed," is derived (the same word used in the Beatitudes). Only twice does the verb *makarizoo* appear in Scripture: in Luke 1:48 in regard to the Virgin Mary who was to bear God's Son: "From henceforth all generations shall call me blessed (*makariousin*)." This means by implication "indwelt by God," which in her case meant that the Lord Jesus, in whom dwelt "all the fulness of the Godhead bodily" (Col. 2:9) was conceived in her by the Holy Spirit. The generations to come would recognize that fact. The second use of this verb is in James 5:11, where James, speaking of the prophets, says, "Behold, we count them blessed (*makarizomen*), those who endured." The word is not "happy" here, as in the King James Version, but "blessed," as the New American Standard Version correctly renders it. Those prophets who endured persecution and privations we consider as being indwelt by God.

If Paul had used *makarizomen* for "bless" in I Corinthians 4:12—"being reviled, we bless"—it would have been completely nonsensical, for it would have meant "we consider them as being indwelt by God." They certainly would not have reviled the apostles if God was in them.

Instead, Paul used the word *eulogoumen,* "we speak well of." The word "speak" here has the connotation of "wish." We are to wish well to someone who reviles us. But the "well" is not necessarily in accordance with what he does or wishes, for if he is a reviler that can only be the continuation of his evil ways. It is rather what we as Christians consider good for our enemies, and that is their salvation in and through Christ.

We don't love our enemies when we permit them to continue in their evil ways, but when we seek to bring about the necessary change in them for good. That change may be brought about by silence or by speech, by forgiveness or by punishment, depending on the person and the circumstances.

The poet Tasso was once told that he had an opportunity to take advantage of a bitter enemy. He replied, "I wish not to plunder him; but there are things I wish to take from him: not his honor, his wealth, or his life, but his malice and ill will."

Similarly the Christian aims, not at getting even with his enemy, but at winning him to Christ and in the process turning him from an enemy to a brother in the Lord.

Should Christians Expect Persecution?

So far we have seen that, when the apostles were persecuted, they accepted physical deprivation and psychological indignities as part of the price they were willing to pay for serving Christ in a hostile world. As the Apostle Paul says, "Being persecuted, we suffer it."

What is the persecution he is referring to? The Greek verb is *diookomenoi,* "being persecuted," in the present participial form, nominative case, plural number, passive voice of the verb *diookoo.* It means to put to flight, to drive away. In this sense it is the people of the unbelieving world who try to drive Christians away from their presence. We are like flies in their ointment. Unbelievers are uncomfortable in the company of dedicated Christians and will do all they can to drive them away. The world very rarely tries to convert the Christian to its godless ways; it just wants to get rid of us so that it can pursue its own way unchecked by our presence.

Paul stated this as a principle in II Timothy 3:12: "All that will live godly in Christ Jesus shall suffer persecution." The same Greek verb is used here, *dioochtheesontai.* Observe how all-inclusive Paul makes this observation—"all." No true Christian living in the world will have it easy. If he or she is truly in Christ, and not a compromiser, the world will make it plain their company is not desired. Persecution or an endeavor to minimize their influence

133

in the world is the common lot of all outspoken godly persons.

Thus, when Paul said, "being persecuted, we suffer it," he was giving the negative statement of his previous positive assertion, "we live godly in Christ." The positive statement might have been interpreted as bragging; hence he chose to state the truth negatively. Those whose life is hid with Christ in God daily feed their souls on the invisible realities of another world.

Why, then, do so few Christians suffer persecution today? May it not be because so few live "godly in Christ Jesus"? The world has not changed its philosophy of antipathy toward the Christian, but in many cases the Christian has become worldly. The result is little or no persecution, because our godliness has been greatly watered down. Henry Ward Beecher hit the nail on the head when he said, "We preach cream and live only skim milk."

When our godliness begins to be felt, when we have the courage of our convictions, and practice what we preach, the world reacts. Lord Peterborough said concerning his contact with the French theologian Fenelon, "He is an energetic creature. I was forced to get away from him as fast as I possibly could, or else he would have made me pious."

A non-Christian lawyer attended a church service and listened incredulously to the testimonies of some who were known to him for their shady deals and failure to meet their honest obligations. "How did you like the testimonies?" a man asked him at the close of the service. He replied, "To a lawyer there is a vast difference between testimony and evidence." Words are cheap, and it is perilously easy to give a fine-sounding testimony for Christ, but quite another matter to demonstrate evidences of God's purifying power in our lives through

Christ. "This people honoureth me with their lips, but their heart is far from me" (Mark 7:6).

Note that the Beatitudes in Matthew 5 give only one verse to each of the individual traits of being poor in spirit, mourning, meekness, hungering after righteousness, mercifulness, purity of heart, and peacemaking. But when it comes to suffering persecution, three verses are employed. In this way the Lord stresses how difficult it is for the world to believe that those who serve Him faithfully are indeed blessed in spite of the world's persecution.

What happens when only one member of a family is converted to Christ? He is often isolated from the rest as a sore thumb. He interferes with their enjoyment of sinful pursuits. That's what the Lord meant when He said that He came to earth, not to bring peace but a sword, indicating that a man's foes would be those of his own household.

Persecution is indeed a criterion of godliness when commitment and dedication to Christ are the cause of it. Why wasn't Judas persecuted? He was with Christ but not in Christ, and Christ was never in him. Look at Mark 10:30, in which Christ makes such extensive promises to those who have left all for Him. In His promise of blessing to them He inserts a word of caution concerning persecution. "But he shall receive an hundredfold now in this time, houses, and brethren, and sisters, and mothers, and children, and lands, with persecutions; and in the world to come eternal life." The word "persecutions" is in the plural number, including all kinds of persecutions.

Our Lord was persecuted from the manger to the cross. He was hated by wicked men, called a blasphemer, a winebibber, a Samaritan, and a devil, and had all manner of evil spoken against Him.

135

Many people separated themselves from His company and were ashamed to be seen with Him openly. They sought to stone Him, thrust Him out of synagogues, arraigned Him as a deceiver of the people. They scourged Him, spit upon Him, and finally crucified Him. Thus did the Lord suffer; and the servant is not above his Lord. "If they have persecuted me, they will also persecute you," He said to His disciples in John 15:20. Christian, if you want to be like your Lord, don't expect to escape suffering and persecution.

Overcoming Evil with Good

Why is it that godly Christians are persecuted? It's because of the incongruity of the natures of the believer and the unbeliever. Ever since the fall there has been an irreconcilable enmity between the seed of the woman and the seed of the serpent, as stated in Genesis 3:15. The woman was Mary, who was to bring forth the Son of Man, Jesus. The serpent is Satan.

Wicked men hate God and therefore cannot help hating those who are like Him. They don't want to be changed and therefore must hate and persecute the servants of Jesus Christ. If they commend them, they are afraid of being asked, "Why don't you follow them?" Though they may sometimes be forced to approve them, yet pride and envy make them persecutors. It has always been true that he who is born after the flesh, the natural man, will persecute him that is born after the Spirit, the regenerate man.

What should the Christian's reaction be? Paul expresses it by the Greek word *anechometha*, "we suffer it or endure it." The verb is in the middle voice, present indicative. We are not forced to suffer persecution; we choose to do so out of love for Christ. It's up to us how we're to face it. We can resist it and counter-attack.

But Paul says the best policy for the Christian is to endure and restrain himself. In Modern Greek the word has come to mean "to tolerate." The English word "tolerance" is derived from the Latin *tolerare,* "to endure, to bear." But does this enduring mean that we cannot defend ourselves against those who try to harm us and others or the cause of Christ?

As Christians we are to love our enemies as ourselves. Therefore if our love for self is the pattern of our love for our enemies, it must be as good as that for our enemies—an extension of the love we have for ourselves. Therefore our attitude toward persecution does not infer careless abandonment of our lives or what belongs to us. If this were the case, then every effort to restrain the evildoer would be unscriptural. We can endure and at the same time do everything in our power to counteract the designs of the evildoers.

The substantive *anochee* (from the verb *anechoo),* "endurance" or "forbearance," is to be distinguished from two other Greek words: *makro-thumia,* "longsuffering," and *hupomonee,* "patience." *Makrothumia* is patience in respect of persons, and *hupomonee* is patience in respect of things. God is said to be longsuffering (*makrothumos*) toward men because He respects the wills that He has given them, even when these wills are fighting against Him. But things cannot resist God; therefore we never read of the patience (*hupomonee*) of God toward things. When God is called the God of patience (*Theos tees hupomonees*) in Romans 15:5, it does not mean that God has the attribute of *hupomonee* or patience toward things, but that He is the God who gives patience to His servants and saints in the same manner as He is spoken of as the God of grace (*Theos charitos*) in I Peter 5:10, the God who is the Author of grace, not the receiver of it.

Now *anochee,* used in its verb form in I Corinthians 4:12, is used of a truce or suspension of arms. It occurs as a substantive twice in the New Testament and is correctly rendered "forbearance" (Rom. 2:4; 3:25). *Anochee* is temporary, transient, just like a truce. It asserts its own temporary, transient character; that after a certain lapse of time, and unless other conditions intervene, it will pass away.

This is true also of *makrothumia,* "longsuffering." The Lord is longsuffering toward us, in spite of what we are. But He is anxious and active in changing us to become what He wants us to be. The Lord never ceases His actions toward changing us. And if we do not change it is entirely our fault. Examine Romans 2:4, in which both *makrothumia* and *anochee* occur: "Or despisest thou the riches of his goodness and forbearance (*anochee*) and longsuffering (*makrothumia*); not knowing that the goodness of God leadeth thee to repentance?" God's forbearance and longsuffering have one aim, the repentance of the sinner. The same truth is seen in Romans 3:25, 26: "Through the forbearance (*anochee*) of God; to declare, I say, at this time his righteousness: that he might be just, and the justifier of him which believeth in Jesus." Again the forbearance (*anochee*) of God leads to belief in Jesus Christ.

This intricate meaning of the verb *anechometha,* "we forbear or endure," throws light upon what Paul means when he says, "being persecuted, we forbear." We endure or tolerate the situation temporarily but not passively. We work with all that is at our disposal in order to change the persecutor, not reacting immediately in such a way that we lose the opportunity of long-range results. Striking back at our persecutors may be necessary in order to protect ourselves and others; but it is up to us to devise long-range plans to change our persecutors. And that's what it means to love our enemies, to be temporarily forbearing of them and work toward changing them to be friends. It is overcoming evil with good, not retaliating in kind, or merely passively enduring evil.

(See *Synonyms of the New Testament,* by R. C. Trench, pp. 195-200; *Sermons Preached upon Several Occasions,* by Robert South, pp. 223-33; *Memoirs of Rev. George Whitefield,* pp. 327-39; and *Theological Dictionary of the New Testament,* by G. Kittel, vols. I, II, and IV.)

When Others Lie about You

"Being defamed, we intreat: we are made as the filth of the world, and are the offscouring of all things unto this day" (I Cor. 4:13).

The Christian Reaction to Slander

One of the hardest things for a Christian to take is slander, especially when he's doing his best to serve the Lord and help others in need. That's one of the tools Satan uses to discourage God's servants. An evil person has no cause for complaint when others speak evil of him, for he has brought it on himself. But it hurts when what others speak of us is sheer falsehood.

In I Corinthians 4:11-13, the Apostle Paul enumerates the sufferings that he and other apostles had to bear because of their witness for Christ. The first sufferings he mentions are physical: hunger, thirst, scant clothing, violent abuse, and uncertain shelter. And last in this list is the fact that, although they had so much spiritual work to do, they had to engage in manual labor to support themselves.

Then, in the middle of verse 12, he speaks of the sufferings they had to endure in the spiritual realm: being reviled and persecuted. Sometimes, of course, persecution may be altogether physical, but here we believe Paul is referring to spiritual persecution, since it occurs between the expressions "being reviled" and "being defamed or blasphemed."

It is this third form of spiritual suffering in the Christian's service and walk that we want to consider now. Verse 13 begins with the present passive participle, nominative masculine plural, of the verb *duspheemeoo: duspheemoumenoi,* "being defamed." The Greek verb is a compound of the particle *dus,* conveying the notion of "untowardness, as hard, ill, unlucky, dangerous," like the English prefixes "un" or "mis." It is the opposite of *eu,* which has a good connotation. We have words prefixed by *eu,* such as *eu*phemism (that which sounds good), and *eu*phony (pleasing or sweet sound).

The other part of the compound verb from which *duspheemeoo* is derived is *pheemi,* "to speak, to utter a sound." This involves our "fame," our good reputation, which is being distorted. The defamer is taking our good name and presenting it to third parties as bad. It is the misrepresentation and butchering of our character to others, behind our backs. This is what is known as slander. It is not a physical thing perpetrated by the hand, but a more subtle form of persecution through the tongue.

In the Beatitudes, our Lord mentions the three evils perpetrated against the Christian in exactly the same order. In Matthew 5:11 we read: "Blessed are ye, when men shall revile you [*oneidisoosin* is used here as a synonym for *loidoroomenoi* in I Corinthians 4:12], and persecute you, and shall say all manner of evil against you falsely, for my sake." That's defaming, more commonly known as slander.

142

We must be careful of two things when we hear that someone has said something derogatory about us:

First, is it true? If it is, then we must admit it and try by God's grace to correct our fault. Note that our Lord stated very clearly that it must be a *false* accusation, if it is to result in the furtherance of our blessedness: "And shall say all manner of evil against you *falsely*."

Second, is it for Christ's sake that we are being defamed? Such defamation may result either from our own endeavors to elevate ourselves and show off, or from our earnest uplifting of Jesus Christ. We can be slandered for "self's" sake or for Christ's sake. If it's for self, our usual reaction is retaliation and countercharges. If it's for Christ's sake, we are to accept it with prayerful concern.

If we are innocent, and the accusations are false, our hearts should be free from fear. The world's unfavorable view of our character and conduct is like the fleeting clouds from which the brightest day is not free, or, to change the metaphor, the mud doesn't stick to the back of a smooth fish. In the same way, slander will not stick to us if we are innocent. In the long run, God will vindicate us. The poet was wise who said,

> Trust not to each accusing tongue,
> As most weak persons do;
> But still believe that story false
> Which ought not to be true.

In a sense, we are prisoners of the slanders leveled against us by those who speak evil of us for Christ's sake. But we can emulate the serenity of that man who stood in the courtroom who seemed to smile at the heavy charges leveled against him. A bystander asked him why he smiled. "Oh," he said, "it makes no difference what the evidence says, as long as the judge says nothing." It is no matter what the world says as long as God approves us.

There's no doubt that slander hurts. There's only a single letter's difference between "words" and "swords." Slanderers are like flies; they light only upon our sores, where they know they will hurt us most. Sir Francis Bacon expressed a profound truth when he said, "The worthiest persons are frequently attacked by slanderers, as we generally find that to be the best fruit which the birds have been pecking at."

When Slander Becomes Blasphemy

The Greek text of the New Testament sheds a great deal of light on the meaning of Scripture. For instance, in I Corinthians 4:13, when the Apostle Paul says, "Being defamed, we intreat," some texts, instead of using the verb *duspheemoumenoi,* "being defamed," as we saw in our previous study, use the verb *blaspheemoumenoi,* "being blasphemed," a far commoner New Testament word.

The noun *duspheemia,* "slander, insult, evil report," is used only in II Corinthians 6:8 besides the verbal usage in I Corinthians 4:13. What is the difference? The verb *blaspheemeoo* is also a compound. It is made up of *blas,* which may be derived either from *blax,* "stupid, sluggish, lazy" (still used in Modern Greek), or from *blaptoo,* "to injure or hurt," and *pheemi,* "to speak." Interesting, isn't it? The one who blasphemes shows himself stupid in trying to injure someone else.

But the word "blaspheme" in the New Testament also took on the connotation of speech defamatory of the Deity and the divine. A blasphemer is thus one who speaks contemptuously of God or of sacred things (as in Matt. 9:3, Mark 3:28, Rom. 2:24, I Tim. 1:20, and Rev. 13:6). The apostles and Christians in general represent God and that which is divine. Therefore when others speak against them it is as if they were speaking against God Himself and the sacred truths for which Christians stand.

What really angers the unbeliever is our claim to a special relationship with God. In a unique sense, this is what made the scribes call Jesus Christ a blasphemer—His claim of a special relationship with God the Father, which even Christian believers do not pretend to have, namely, equality in Deity with God the Father. "But there were certain of the scribes sitting there, and reasoning in their hearts, Why doth this man thus speak blasphemies? who can forgive sins but God only?" (Mark 2:6, 7, Luke 5:20, 21, Matt. 9:2, 3). Their reasoning was clear: Christ presumed to forgive sins. Only God could do that. Therefore, by so doing, Christ claimed to be God, and that was blasphemy!

What Jesus had done was to give an explicit assertion of His special relationship to God the Father. He demonstrated that He had power to speak the authoritative word of forgiveness because of His perfect oneness with the Father, in mind and will and purpose. When was it that the people took up stones to throw at Him? When He said, "I and my Father are one" (John 10:30). The Greek word for "one" here is *hen,* in substance, in divinity, in essence; not one personality, as could have been expressed by the Greek *heis.*

The Lord asked them, "Many good works have I shewed you from my Father; for which of those works do you stone me? The Jews answered him, saying, For a good work we stone thee not; but for blasphemy; and because that thou, being a man, makest thyself God" (John 10:32, 33).

Even the Christian's claim to a special rela-

145

tionship to Christ as Saviour, and thus to God as Father, seems almost like blasphemy to the world. Our beliefs are repugnant to the natural mind. Therefore they call us fools, idiots, and worse. Paul wants us to be prepared for this by realizing that our defamation by the unbelieving world has its basis in our special relationship with God as His redeemed children.

What was Paul's reaction, and that of the other apostles, to this? "Being defamed, we intreat," he said. The rendering in the Authorized Version doesn't fully convey the thought here. The New American Standard Version says, "we try to conciliate," and the New International Version says, "we answer kindly." Let's see what the Greek verb *parakaloumen* really means. It comes from *parakaleoo,* a compound verb made up of the preposition *para,* "near, to the side," and the verb *kaleoo,* "to call." Hence it can mean to invite someone, to appeal to, urge, exhort, encourage, request, implore. It also means to comfort, to encourage, or to cheer up. It is in this latter sense that the word is used in the second Beatitude in Matthew 5:4, "Blessed the mourning ones, for they shall be comforted [*parakleetheesontai*]." He who mourns needs someone to stand by his side, to comfort him.

But in I Corinthians 4:13 the verb is used in the active voice, *parakaloumen,* "we stand by, we beseech." To whom do we do this? It cannot be the one who has defamed or blasphemed us. It is doubtful that such a person would want us by his side, either to speak to us or have us speak to him. His work of ruining our reputation is usually done in our absence, to a third party. In this way we are left defenseless, as he poisons the minds of others against us.

The verb *parakaloumen* in this instance has its

own peculiar meaning. If we take its object to be God, then it can mean "We beseech or entreat God," in other words, "We pray, we stand by God." The word is used with the meaning of "pray" and is so translated in Matthew 26:53, where it is used in relation to the proclamation of salvation. What do we do, then, when we hear of someone slandering us because of our relationship to Jesus Christ? We beseech God for his salvation. That's the only way the slanderer may be stopped. We seek to be reconciled to him, not on the basis of sacrificing truth and principle, or even with a defense of our integrity, but on the basis of much entreaty, much prayer for his salvation.

"Love Your Enemies . . . Pray for Them

When we think of slander, we usually associate it with the tongue. But do we ever stop to think we may be guilty of it simply by lending our ears?

Some young women were talking about one of their friends, when their pastor happened to enter the room. He overheard the epithets "odd," "singular," and other belittling words applied to the absent friend. The pastor asked about whom they were talking, and then commented, "Yes, she is an odd young lady, a very odd young lady; I consider her extremely singular." He then added very impressively, "She was never heard to speak ill of an absent friend." The rebuke struck home.

We must remember that we are guilty of assisting in the work of defamation when we allow someone to speak ill of an absent person to us. The slanderer wounds three at once: himself, the one he speaks of, and the one that hears. If we cannot stop his mouth, let us stop our ears. For as soon as we take pleasure in hearing slander we are ranked among the number of those who engage in slander.

147

As Bishop Hall said, "There would not be so many open mouths if there were not so many open ears." And Leighton adds, "Calumny would soon starve and die of itself if nobody took it in and gave it lodging." Proverbs 26:20 puts it succinctly: "Where no wood is, there the fire goeth out: so where there is no talebearer, the strife ceaseth."

But what shall we do when slander becomes extremely personal? How can we stop those who are defaming us? Perhaps one way we can get to our enemies is to say something good about them.

General Lee was once asked by military authorities about the merits and qualifications of an officer who had been particularly unkind to him, stooping even to slander and backbiting. The General, always a Christian and a gentleman, made an exceedingly favorable report. "What do you mean, General?" a friend asked him. "Don't you know how much harm that man has done you?" "I am well aware of this," was the dignified reply, "but you forget that I have been asked, not concerning what he thinks of me, but concerning what I think of him."

As Christians we must ever keep in mind what our Lord taught us in Matthew 5:44: "Love your enemies, bless them that curse you, do good to them that hate you, and pray for them which despitefully use you, and persecute you." Slander, defamation, and blasphemy is one kind of persecution. By telling us to love our enemies, the Lord doesn't mean we are to face them with honey-coated words that are the opposite of what we feel in our heart. That would be hypocrisy. We must rid our mind of all resentment and hatred toward them. Through acts of kindness we must try to meet their real needs. But what will really meet their need is prayer to God for their salvation. By prayer we acknowledge that words and deeds of kindness on our part are insufficient to change them. We need the intervention of the omnipotent God to bring salvation.

What do we as Christians see in the person who hates or defames us: an enemy only, or also a fellow human being for whom Christ died? If my enemy were a poisonous snake, it might be justifiable for me to hate and trample upon him. But am I justified in hating the seed of the woman as much as I do that of the serpent? God loves the most sinful members of the human race, so far as their being His creatures. Enmity does not obliterate humanity. Every man may see something of himself in his enemy, and must believe that an enemy is capable of being shamed and redeemed.

The scribes and Pharisees were defaming Jesus; they were His enemies. He didn't blind His eyes to them; He recognized them for what they were. That's what we must do if we are to help our enemies. The right diagnosis is the prerequisite to proper treatment. The Lord did not meekly avoid a confrontation with them, for this would have emboldened them to continue their evil attitudes and actions. He opposed them with all His strength. But at the same time He prayed for them. So ought we to pray that our enemies will see the error of their ways and repent.

Read the 23rd chapter of Matthew, and notice how the Lord first told the Pharisees what He thought of them. "Woe unto you, scribes and Pharisees, hypocrites! for ye shut up the kingdom of heaven against men: for ye neither go in yourselves, neither suffer ye them that are entering to go in. . . . ye devour widows' houses, and for a pretence make long prayer: therefore ye shall receive greater damnation" (vv. 13, 14; see also 23, 24).

He didn't hold anything back. This was exposure upon exposure, when exposure was necessary. He spoke the truth for the protection of others and to jolt them out of their self-righteous complacency. But He didn't stop with denunciation. In effect He prayed for them: "O Jerusalem, Jerusalem, thou that killest the prophets, and stonest them which are sent unto thee, how often would I have gathered thy children together, even as a hen gathereth her chickens under her wings, and ye would not! Behold, your house is left unto you desolate. For I say unto you, Ye shall not see me henceforth, till ye shall say, Blessed is he that cometh in the name of the Lord" (vv. 38, 39). This presupposes their repentance, of course.

Be Willing to Take It

Have you ever been deeply hurt because someone you loved and trusted turned against you? If so, you're in good company. Consider what Judas did to Jesus Christ. But before you begin thinking of your false friend as another Judas, and become bitter and revengeful, consider how Jesus acted.

Who defamed Jesus more than His traitorous disciple, Judas? Yet consider what the Lord did at the last supper. See Him kneeling at the traitor's feet, washing and wiping them with the same marks of love and tenderness He bestowed on the other disciples. When Judas follows Him to the garden of Gethsemane, what does the Lord do? He accepts his treacherous kiss and salutes him with the name of friend.

Now accompany the Saviour to the palaces of Annas and Caiaphas. In the one He receives a blow on the cheek; in the other His enemies buffet Him and spit in His face. He rebukes them but does not return blow for blow, or insult for insult.

On to Calvary. On the cross He neither heaps curses on His enemies nor calls down vengeance upon them. On the contrary, He lifts His eyes to Heaven and prays for them to be forgiven. Dare we, as His servants, do otherwise?

The Apostle Paul was of the same spirit as his Master. In concluding the list of sacrifices he and other apostles were making for Christ's sake, he says in the second part of I Corinthians 4:13, "We are made as the filth of the world, and are the offscouring of all things unto this day."

Up to now Paul has been using the present indicative or present participial forms of verbs. "We are hungry, we are thirsty, we are scantily dressed, we are mistreated, we are without an abiding house, we labor working with our own hands, being reviled, being persecuted, being defamed." But in the conclusion he changes the verbal form by using the aorist tense. Why?

Up to now he has been describing the continuous state of the apostles. It was one of privation and persecution. "We are constantly experiencing these things," he says in effect. "But now we have had it; that is what we became for Christ's sake." The verb here is *egeneetheemen,* from *ginomai,* "to become." It's in the aorist tense, which means "we have been made." Made what? A heap of rubbish. By whom? Those who hate the Gospel, as a result of the nature of the work we've been trying to accomplish. The apostles could have had a much easier life had they wanted to accomplish less for the Lord. Their accomplishments for God were proportionate to their willingness to sacrifice. It was not only the enmity of the world but also their love for the Saviour and the souls of men that made them so deprived.

"We are willing to take it," Paul intimates;

although he elsewhere makes it clear that Christians should not allow Christ's servants to fall into abject poverty. That is to their shame. In writing to the Corinthians in II Corinthians 8:14, he rebukes them for having so much, yet giving so little. "Now," he writes, "your abundance may be a supply for their want, that their abundance also may be a supply for your want; that there may be equality."

If a Christian community can supply the needs of Christian workers, they should do so, in order that those who serve the Lord may not have to say, "We go hungry, thirsty, scantily clad," and so on. But no Christian worker should be unwilling to endure these privations for the sake of Christ. No Christian should shirk his responsibility in giving, and no Christian should give up working for God because he may have to suffer deprivation as a result. When Christians fail to support God's work, this does not give license to God's servants to give up their God-commissioned duty.

"We were made the filth of the world," says Paul. The genitive *tou kosmou,* "of the world," has by paraphrase the meaning of "in the eyes of the world." The other genitive, *pantoon,* "of all," in the phrase, "the offscouring of all," should also be taken by paraphrase as "in the eyes of all people." Both expressions refer to unbelievers, who are to a great extent the cause of much of the suffering of God's servants. In their eyes, Paul declares, we are rubbish, offscouring, not worth anything. These are the most debasing terms he could apply to himself and other sacrificing apostles.

There is still a great deal of this sort of persecution going on in the world. In every city there are shops and offices and factories where anyone giving a consistent Christian witness by word and example is ridiculed and subjected to petty annoyances and harassment. And there are homes in which, under the safe cover of what ought to be the most loving relationships, the stabs of aversion and contempt are dealt to the one who faithfully proclaims allegiance to Christ.

Never shrink from wholehearted commitment to the Saviour because you fear its trials or its sacrifices. Remember that Paul in martyrdom was far happier than God's halfhearted servants.

God's Not Through with You Yet

The insults that the Apostle Paul and other apostles had to bear for the sake of their faithful Christian testimony are seen to be even more debasing in the original Greek than in our English translations. The two words that appear in the Authorized Version as "filth" and "offscouring" are *perikatharmata* and *peripseema*. The uncompounded *katharma* (singular) is more common. *Peri* as a prefix means "around." *Katharma,* used even today in Modern Greek, is the worst name anybody could be called. Both words refer to the "sweepings" or "scrapings" scoured off in cleansing a vessel. Neither word occurs elsewhere in the New Testament.

Demosthenes addressed Aeshines as *hoo katharma* (vocative), a term of deepest insult. In another reference, he called some people *katharmata,* "scourings," *kai ptoochoi,* and "poor" (helpless ones) and not even men (*kai oude anthroopoi*). The term denoted helpless creatures, less than human beings. *Perikatharmata* is plural, denoting the sweepings that are gathered together from all around (*peri*).

The second term, *peripseema,* is singular in number and means "offscouring," that which is removed by scouring or rubbing away (*psaoo*) a fil-

153

thy object. Both terms refer to that which is worthless. Paul is saying, "We have become the scum of the earth, the refuse of the world," as the New International Version renders it in paraphrase. "We are not worth anything to the world up until now."

That phrase "until now" is very important. It refers to the whole paragraph from verses 11 through 13. All the sufferings that Paul and the other apostles were willing to undergo for the sake of Christ were temporary. A brighter day would dawn. The era in which we now live is the day of man; but the Lord's day will come, in which He will wipe away all tears. Revelation 7:17 says of the righteous ones, "And God shall wipe away all tears from their eyes." Isaiah 25:8 says, "He will swallow up death in victory; and the Lord God will wipe away tears from off all faces; and the rebuke of his people shall he take away from off all the earth: for the Lord hath spoken it." And again, in Isaiah 35:10 we read, "And the ransomed of the Lord shall return, and come to Zion with songs and everlasting joy upon their heads: they shall obtain joy and gladness, and sorrow and sighing shall flee away." (See also 51:11; 60:20.)

"Till now," said Paul as he remembered God's promise in Psalm 30:5: "Weeping may endure for a night, but joy cometh in the morning." And the last book of the Bible gives an assurance that enables the believer to endure joyfully all kinds of suffering: "And God shall wipe away all tears from their eyes; and there shall be no more death, neither sorrow, nor crying, neither shall there be any more pain: for the former things are passed away" (Rev. 21:4).

The Lord is not through with us yet. He is still in the process of making and molding us through experiences of joy and suffering. Before the war destroyed it, in a certain town in France there was a curiously wrought crucifix. It gave the spectator two totally different impressions when seen from different angles of vision. Seen from one point of view, the Saviour's face was full of beauty; from another it was marred with cruel disfigurements. From one standpoint it was calm and peaceful, as though Christ were looking up into His Father's face and saying, "Father, into thy hands I commit my spirit." From another standpoint it wore a look of anguish, as though He were crying, "My God, my God, why hast thou forsaken me?" Standing in one place you would see the face of Jesus as one "rejoicing in spirit" (Luke 10:21); standing elsewhere you would see the same face as the index of a soul in deep sorrow: "Now is my soul troubled" (John 12:27).

In many ways the persecuted apostles mirrored this dual experience: "As sorrowful, yet alway rejoicing" (II Cor. 6:10). God was not through with them yet, and this was all part of His making and molding process. And that explains much of the seemingly mysterious providences of His dealings with us.

A happily married woman with two children lost both of them. They were buried in the same grave, and she went into a deep emotional collapse. For some years she became as helpless as a little child. She had to be fed by members of her family, who ministered to her.

One day as her aunt, who was a joyful Christian, took her turn at feeding her, this woman who was unusually despondent that morning said, "Oh, Auntie, you say that God loves us. You say it, and you keep on saying it. I used to think that way, too, but if He loves us, why did He make me as I am?"

And the aunt, after kissing her gently, said

with the wisdom of the years, "He hasn't made you yet, child. He's making you now!"

When through fiery trials thy pathway shall lie,
My grace, all-sufficient, shall be thy supply;
The flame shall not hurt thee; I only design
Thy dross to consume and thy gold to refine.

Conduct Resulting from Conviction

"I write not these things to shame you, but as my beloved sons I warn you" (I Cor. 4:14).

The Blessing of Sacrificing for Christ

The Corinthians were evidently wealthy Christians for the most part. They gave but they did not sacrifice. It was easy for them to compromise with the world around them, and thus escape scornful reproach. They had an easy time of it; persecution was not their lot. Unlike the apostles, they seldom if ever had to hunger and thirst for Christ's sake.

That was the choice they had made: the life of ease while still being in Christ. They were the rich who were not willing to become poor for Christ's sake. I Corinthians 4:8 shows us what an easy time they had of it: "Now ye are full, now ye are rich, ye have reigned as kings without us." Then Paul goes on to describe what he and the other apostles were enduring up till that time.

157

It was only natural that Paul's words should cause the Corinthians a sense of shame. "Look how good we have it, and what a hard time those poor preachers are having." But that was the last thing Paul wanted to inculcate in them. "I write not these things to shame you," he says in I Corinthians 4:14.

The Greek word translated "shame" here is *entrepoon,* the present participle of *entrepoo,* a compound verb made up of the preposition *en,* meaning "in," and *trepoo,* "to turn." There are three Greek words that are translated "shame" in English. There is the noun *aischunee,* which expresses that feeling that leads one to shun what is unworthy for fear of incurring dishonor. It is as though we realize our imperfections and are grieved, but our grief is not because of our shortcomings but because of what other people will think who take notice of them.

As a noun, this word is used in Luke 14:9, II Corinthians 4:2 (translated "dishonesty"), Philippians 3:19, Hebrews 12:2, Jude 13, and Revelation 3:18. As a verb it is used in Luke 16:3, II Corinthians 10:8, Philippians 1:20, I Peter 4:26, and I John 2:28. With the preposition *epi,* "on," as *epaischunomai* it is used in Mark 8:38, Luke 9:26, Romans 1:16; 6:21, II Timothy 1:8, 12, 16, and Hebrews 2:11; 11:16.

Take the well-known verse of Romans 1:16: "For I am not ashamed of the gospel of Christ." It means "I do not realize a sense of shame when others recognize that I am a Christian." This shame is coupled with what others will think of us when they learn of a certain thing we do or believe.

The second Greek word translated "shame" is *aidoos,* used only in I Timothy 2:9. It means the shame that finds its motive in itself, that is, modesty, propriety. No honor and reputation are attached to this sense of shame. We are not ashamed because of what others think of us, but because of the regard we have for our own self or for goodness and God. Thus it could be said that *aischunee* would sometimes restrain a bad person, while *aidoos* would always restrain a good person from an unworthy act.

Entropee is the word used in I Corinthians 4:14 in its verbal participial form: "I write these things not shaming you [*entrepoon*]." As a verb it occurs in Matthew 21:37 and Mark 12:6, where it means "respect or regard," Luke 18:2, 4; 20:13, where it also means "respect or regard," and in I Corinthians 4:14, II Thessalonians 3:14, and Titus 2:8, where it means "shame." As a noun it occurs only twice: in I Corinthians 6:5 and 15:34.

Entropee is rendered "shame" as is *aischunee* and *aidoos,* but it has something in it that neither of these two words has. It conveys at least a hint of a change of conduct. It means "a return upon oneself"; it involves a change in conduct as one turns upon himself. That was what Paul was hoping would happen as he wrote to the Corinthians about their material riches and ease and his own privations and sufferings for Christ. His aim was not simply to produce a sense of shame in them as a result of what he and the other apostles thought of them, nor because of what they thought of themselves, but to cause them to turn upon themselves for the purpose of changing their conduct. (See R. C. Trench, *Synonyms of the New Testament,* pp. 66-9.)

Entropee in Classical Greek may mean "respect or reverence for one," as well as "shame or reproach"; the context determines which. The verb *entrepoo* in the passive form may mean "to respect, to regard, to reverence, to pay deference to (anyone)."

We should never try to shame others for their conduct that we find unbecoming to the principles we have set for ourselves. But if we really believe that our conduct is exemplary, we should endeavor to show others the superiority of our way with the motive of changing their conduct. That was Paul's purpose as he spells it out in I Corinthians 4:16 by saying, "Wherefore I beseech you, be ye followers of me." He knew the blessing of sacrificing for Christ's sake, and he didn't want them to miss such a blessing.

A fable tells of a little piece of wood that once complained bitterly because its owner kept whittling away at it, cutting it and filling it with holes. But the one who was cutting it so remorselessly paid no attention to its complaining. He was making a flute out of that piece of ebony, and he was too wise to give up because the wood moaned so piteously. His actions seemed to say, "Little piece of wood, without these holes and all this cutting, you would be a black stick forever—just a useless piece of ebony. What I am doing now may make you think that I am destroying you, when actually I am changing you into a flute, whose sweet music will comfort sorrowing hearts. My cutting you is the making of you, for only thus can you be a blessing to the world."

Right Motives for a Change of Conduct

When the Apostle Paul wrote to the Corinthian Christians of the deprivations he and the other apostles were suffering for the cause of Christ, while the Corinthians were living at ease, he did it because he saw they needed correction, a change of conduct. But there was really nothing he himself could do to bring this about. Sharp words and criticism bring shame, but they do not necessarily cause a change in conduct and attitude. They may make a person "turn in" (*entrepoo*) on himself, resulting in some change, but such a change is accompanied by

160

resentment. It is not a joyful change resulting from conviction.

We can change our conduct if we have to, in order to survive in a world in which people are prone to shame and ridicule us for behavior of which they disapprove. Our attitude may change only because we want to avoid being treated with contempt. This is a hypocritical change of attitude, not of character. We act differently from the way we wish we could if we were not afraid of incurring the displeasure of others.

That was not the kind of change Paul wanted to bring about in the Corinthians' conduct. Take generosity as an example. Paul touches upon this in II Corinthians 8:1-5. He contrasts the giving of the Corinthians with the sacrificial giving of the Macedonians. The Corinthians gave, not because they wanted to, but because the sacrificial giving of the Macedonians, although insignificant in quantity, made them ashamed. Paul didn't want them to change on that account, but out of conviction that giving carried in itself a blessing, as our Lord taught when He said that it was more blessed to give than to receive. Thus we can be givers out of shame or out of conviction. Which kind are you?

That's why Paul writes to the Corinthians, "I do not write these things in order to shame you," that is, to make you "turn your eyes inside you" (*entrepoon*) for the purpose of bringing about a superficial and hypocritical change in your attitude. The principle verb here is *graphoo*, "I write," and the verb "shame" is in the present active participial form (*entrepoon*). Paul reveals the underlying purpose of his writing—not just to let off steam but to accomplish something. Far too many people write or speak in order to cause others to do as they do, without any personal conviction or real change of character. Do we try to shame people into a position they do not believe in? That was never the purpose of apostolic preaching, writing, or teaching, and it should not be ours. It disregards entirely the work of the Holy Spirit, and puts us in the position of "playing God."

From the negative Paul moves on to the positive. "I do not write in order to shame you, but as my children [who are] beloved I admonish you." The word "admonish" here is *noutheteoo* in Greek. It is derived from the noun *nous,* "mind," and the verb *titheemi,* "to place." If we were to translate the verb literally, we could render Paul's statement, "I place your mind in its proper place"; in other words, I make you think rightly; and only as a result of this can I expect the hoped-for change in your conduct. I want you to be like me, a sacrificial Christian, but only as a result of self-examination and conviction. Your action must be the result of your thought—not to avoid shame in relation to others, but for the purpose of satisfying God who has set your thought process aright. I am doing this, Paul declares, because I consider you my children who are beloved to me. I am your spiritual father.

Isn't this how a loving father acts? Does he want his children to be puppets, merely acting good before others in order to avoid bringing shame upon themselves and him? No, he wants his counsel to affect their minds so they can think for themselves in order to determine what is right and wrong, and then to be able to choose between what is merely right and what is excellent.

Translated, that could be called "nouthetic" counseling, that which rectifies the thinking processes, rather than merely causes action for the purpose of avoiding shame as a form of punishment. The latter is avoiding the consequences of evil, while the former is avoiding the evil itself simply because it is evil, and not just out of fear of the consequences. When we reach that elevated position of thinking (*nouthesia,* the noun form of the verb *nouthetein*), we have really arrived at the stature of Christ. If we love our children, our aim will be not simply to make them follow our example, but to cause them to think that we are worthy of being followed. They will not do what we do simply because that's the way we expect them to act, but because that's the way they themselves think and consequently believe to be proper behavior.

As Kenneth W. Sollitt says in the last three lines of his poem, "God Must Be Like That":

For something in [Christ's] godliness
Has gripped the soul of me —
And I would be like that.

Christian Maturity a Matter of Growth

An easy mistake for Christian parents to fall into is to seek to make their children carbon copies of themselves. But, if we really love our children, we will want them to learn to think things through for themselves, and be able to act out of conviction rather than merely parroting our convictions.

The Apostle Paul truly loved the Corinthian Christians. He does not merely refer to the fact that they were his children in the Lord, but that they were "beloved" children. The word for "children" in I Corinthians 4:14 is *tekna,* from the verb *tiktoo,* "to give birth to." Paul indeed gave birth to these Christians, in the sense that it was through his preaching that they were born into the family of God through faith in Christ.

But one can give birth to a child without necessarily exercising love toward that child. That was not Paul's way. He not only gave spiritual birth to the Corinthians, but he also loved them. That is why he words his counsel to them in a way that will lead them to think aright, and in so doing to act as their spiritual father.

The adjective Paul uses to express his love is one of apposition. He says, "but as my children, beloved ones [*agapeeta*]." He could have used another Greek word, such as *pephileemena,* from *phileoo,* which denotes the love of equals having common interests. But he doesn't; he uses the adjective derived from *agapaoo,* which may express the love of the superior for the inferior, not for the sake of taking advantage of the person who is the object of love, but for the sake of helping him.

This is a beautiful example of Christian grace. The Corinthians could very easily have misunderstood what Paul meant when he wrote to them about a life of sacrifice and privation. They might have concluded that he was trying to get them to help him financially. He wanted to avoid giving that impression, for it was the farthest thing from his mind. He was not admonishing them for his own sake or benefit, but for their sakes, so that they might realize that there is inherent blessing in living a life of sacrifice and privation for the sake of Jesus Christ.

God Himself does not love us for His own personal gain. He doesn't want us to give so that He can have more, but so that we may experience a joy that we couldn't have in any other way. A truly loving father doesn't admonish his children so that he may be served and lack nothing, but so that they will grow up to think right and act right. A loving father does what he does for his children, and counsels them, primarily because he wants to help them to become mature, wise adults. Children can easily see through a person whose counseling has a selfish motive and will comply only as long as they are forced to. Then, when the bonds of necessity cease to exist, the bonds of filial obedience will be terminated.

What Paul wrote to the Corinthian Christians was to make them think right about the blessing of a sacrificial life of faith for the sake of Jesus Christ. To be motivated to such sacrifice, Christians must be convicted and inspired from above, not merely shamed into it for the sake of avoiding embarrassment.

Paul didn't want the Corinthians to think of him as a teacher who was merely doing his duty in instructing them about what was right. "I am not a mere teacher in my relationship with you," he says in effect; "I am a father who loves you. One can have many teachers, but only a single father." He wanted that singular relationship to be realized by the Corinthians. He knew it in his own heart. He loved them; therefore he wanted them to learn to think right in their attitude toward the material things of this world. Hence his words in I Corinthians 4:15: "For if you have ten thousand teachers in Christ, yet have you not many fathers."

He refers to spiritual teachers, for he uses his favorite expression, "in Christ." He recognizes that the Christian life is one of growth and not of instant maturity. Upon being born again, we are "babes in Christ." Just as in our natural life we must first learn how to speak, then how to write, then how to reason, and each age has its proper teachers, something similar takes place in our spiritual life. Just as we wouldn't attempt to teach integral and differential calculus to a child of seven, we shouldn't expect the babe in Christ to grasp all that is implied in Christian doctrine and its outworking in daily life and actions all at once. If we could only realize this principle in our own experience and the lives of others, we wouldn't have so many frustrated pupils. Frustration can come in two ways: through teaching a baby what he can neither understand nor learn, and teaching an adult what is suitable for an infant.

One of the greatest misfortunes in the Christian Church today is the lack of growth evidenced in its members. As one pastor put it in a letter to me, "In most of our churches the Christians are constantly fed pablum, baby food, instead of food for grown-ups."

As someone else has truly observed, "You are only young once, but you can stay immature indefinitely."

Are You a Mere Teacher or a Spiritual Parent?

"For though ye have ten thousand instructors in Christ, yet have ye not many fathers: for in Christ Jesus I have begotten you through the gospel" (I Cor. 4:15).

The Function of Christian Teachers and Fathers

In referring to "ten thousand instructors in Christ," the Apostle Paul was indicating the great multiplicity of teachers in the Christian Church. The number is hypothetical, of course, for effect. But we do need a great many teachers for the various stages of spiritual schooling and growth. No one teacher is fully qualified to teach all the classes in the school of Christ. It is better to divide up our pupils according to their capacity and our ability to teach.

Some teachers in the Christian Church cannot go beyond the ABC's. They are fine for teaching children, or babes in Christ, but cannot reach those on the college level, spiritually speaking. Teacher, find out what spiritual grade you can teach and stick to it. Let those qualified to teach other stages do it.

In this connection, a word of warning. Let's

not presume that because some Christians are in the first grade, so to speak, they are not "in Christ." Observe what Paul says: "For if you have ten thousand teachers in Christ." "In Christ" there are all kinds of pupils, from kindergarten to graduate students. We need discernment to recognize the grade to which each belongs. The temptation may be to consider the weak, carnal, baby Christians as not really "in Christ" at all, and so miss the privilege of helping them grow. Let us heed Paul's admonition in Romans 15:1: "We then that are strong ought to bear the infirmities of the weak, and not to please ourselves." A realistic way of looking at this matter is to recognize that there is always someone who knows less than you do, and you can teach him; and that there is always someone who knows more than you do, who can teach you. We have pupils in all grades in the school of Christ and teachers for all grades. Know yourself and then start teaching and learning.

The word used for teachers ("instructors" in the King James Version) is *paidagoogous,* from the noun *pais,* meaning "child," and the verb *agoo,* "to lead." From this Greek word we derive the English words pedagogue and pedagogy. Teachers are leaders of children for the most part. Paul refuses to classify himself merely as a teacher of children, a pedagogue, in his relationship to the Corinthian Christians. Perhaps by using this term, however, he was implying that the Corinthians were still babes, children in their Christian walk and understanding. In fact, he has already told them so in I Corinthians 3:1-3: "And I, brethren, could not speak unto you as unto spiritual, but as unto babes in Christ. I have fed you with milk, and not with meat: for hitherto ye were not able to bear it, neither yet now are ye able. For ye are yet carnal. . . ."

A teacher is usually a stranger to those whom he teaches. He is appointed by the state or the community or the parents to teach the children. There is no blood relationship that would insure affection between teacher and students, as there is between father and child. The relationship is one of duty on the part of the teacher, and of need on the part of the child. Paul felt that he was more than a teacher, and, though he was actually one of the teachers, he was their only spiritual father.

In our lifetime we need many teachers, but we have only one father who cares for all the phases of our life. He is qualified for this distinct and unique relationship, not because he will always know more than his child does, but simply because at one time he begot him. "But you don't have many fathers," Paul says. He may have been implying that Apollos, for instance, who followed him as a minister in Corinth, would be classified as one of their myriad teachers, but in spite of his brilliance he could not qualify as a spiritual father because he did not beget them. "For in Christ Jesus through the Gospel I gave birth to you," Paul says in effect. "I introduced you to the Gospel first. That and my consistent love for you as my children in Christ qualified me as your spiritual father."

The verb "I gave birth to you" is *egenneesa* in Greek. It is in the aorist tense, which refers to a particular time in the past. Paul claims his spiritual fatherhood on the ground of his having been the first one effectively to bring the Gospel to them. No matter how many taught these Corinthian Christians afterwards, they were never to forget what Paul had done for them, and the special relationship that resulted.

Of course, this does not mean that he was responsible for their salvation, but simply that he was used as God's instrument in the mystery of bringing forth a new spiritual life. A man can be said to beget or father a child, and a woman to give birth; but in reality all that the parents do is to follow the God-prescribed method of procreation. The method and the results have been pre-set and predetermined by God, the Author of all life. Birth is a mystery in the physical world and an even greater mystery in the spiritual world. As Eugenia Price expressed it, "I found I was not only converted, but I was invaded." And that invasion is the very life of Christ in the soul.

Christian Character Dependent upon the New Birth

When the Apostle Paul writes to the Corinthian Christians, "I gave birth to you through the gospel," he is setting forth God's prescribed method. This was not something he did by the force of his own personality; it was his proclamation of the Gospel, energized by the Holy Spirit, that resulted in spiritual children being born in Corinth. Without the Gospel, the good news that Jesus died for sinners and that we are saved by faith in His atoning sacrifice, there would have been no spiritual children brought to birth in Corinth. Let us be faithful in preaching the Gospel; it's "the power of God unto salvation" (Rom. 1:16).

However, when we've brought spiritual children into the world, we are not merely to act as teachers to them, but as fathers. This is not to minimize the efforts of dedicated teachers; but the relationship of fathers is so much closer and dearer. No one could and should have the same affectionate interest in them as we who first brought the Gospel to them. A parent sustains the relationship of affection, mutual help, and caring, in spite of the fact that he may no longer be able to teach the child.

That child, grown to manhood or womanhood, may be a graduate student or a professor in theology, yet he should never cease to look up to his spiritual father. He may know more than he does, but the example and experience of the father are something he may never equal. In addition, there is a great debt of gratitude owed to that person who first led us to the Lord.

A teacher has comparatively few rights over his pupils, but a father has many rights and expectations. So do the children, for that matter. The relationship of teacher-pupil usually ends with the termination of the lesson or the course of study; but the relationship of father-child is an everlasting one, in time and for eternity. I am speaking, of course, of born-again fathers and children. However, even on the purely human level, the father expects respect from his children, and the children expect concern on the part of their father, which may not characterize the teacher-pupil relationship.

There is an innate similarity in the make-up of the children because of the father, which may not hold true in the pupil-teacher relationship. Paul speaks of himself as "father" more often than teacher because he wants his character to be mirrored in the Corinthians; he specifically tells them to follow his example, to be followers of him "as I also am of Christ" (I Cor. 11:1; see also 4:16, and Phil. 3:17).

At this stage of their spiritual development, however, the Corinthians were far from mirroring the character of Paul. He was so sacrificing in his manner of life, they so careless, selfish, and extravagant. "You are full, you have already become rich, you are like kings . . . but we are at the bottom of the ladder, ready to die; we are ridiculed,

171

we are considered insane for the sacrifices we are making; we are sick and weak; but you are strong and famous. We are without fame; hungry, thirsty, ill-clad, buffeted, and have no place we can call home." That, in effect, is the contrast Paul presents to the Corinthians in verses 8-13.

And yet, in verse 15, he declares, "I am your father; I gave birth to you. I am not one of ten thousand teachers. Usually, as fathers and children, we should be characterized by the same qualities, but we are not. Usually it is not the father who imitates the children, but the other way around." All this and more is what Paul implies in verse 15. He gives them to understand that though they were his spiritual children, they didn't evidence it in their every-day conduct. They were compromising for the sake of an easy life, while he was suffering for the sake of Christ.

The unlikeness of character between him as a father and them as his spiritual children must have greatly hurt and embarrassed him. Look at your own spiritual father (and here I am speaking in a general sense, for there are Christian mothers who are worthy to be respected and emulated also). How like him are you? In Galatians 4:19 Paul expresses the grief of a father's heart at the slowness of heart of those who failed to grasp the most elemental facts of law versus grace in the Christian life. "My little children, of whom I travail in birth again until Christ be formed in you," he laments over them. He is not speaking of a mere matter of teaching them to be like Christ, but of giving birth to them. "I gave birth to you through the Gospel," he tells the Corinthians.

The character of Christ is only formed in us as Christ Himself is born in us. No one can learn to be like Christ; he has to be born again, and then Christ enters into him. It is a blood relationship, when, through the efficacy of Christ's blood shed for us, we are cleansed from our sins, and by faith in Him as the Son of God are adopted as sons and daughters into the family of God. The Gospel alone is the power of God that can regenerate in man a truly Christlike character.

What Kind of Example Are You Setting?

Although Scripture expressly states that it is the Gospel that is "the power of God unto salvation" (Rom. 1:16), God employs human instrumentalities also in the regeneration of human souls. The Apostle Paul was not being egotistical when he told the Corinthian Christians, "I gave birth to you." In fact, he uses the personal pronoun *egoo,* from which we derive the English word egotism. The "I" of the verb could have been implied merely by adding the suffix *sa,* i.e., *egenneesa.* But Paul added the personal pronoun *egoo,* "I."

Why did Paul stress the personal element here? Certainly not to show off, but to intimate that, if he had not come to them at the end of his difficult second missionary journey, the Corinthians would probably not have heard the Gospel and might never have become born-again children of God. Paul felt a sense of satisfaction and gratitude to God that his labor of love had not gone in vain.

I certainly believe in the sovereignty of God, but at the same time I believe that He has laid on me the responsibility to preach the Gospel to every creature I possibly can. God can effect His purposes alone, and He still does; but while I am around He expects me to preach the Gospel.

A Christian girl fell in love with a missionary. Before he left for India, he wrote and asked her to become his wife. "If I do not hear from you, I'll know you have other plans," he wrote. She immediately sat down and wrote an acceptance of his proposal. She gave the letter to her brother to mail, but it was never mailed, and she never heard from the missionary again. Years later she found her letter in the lining of her brother's coat, yellow and crumpled. It had slipped there through a hole in the pocket lining, and the brother had forgotten all about it.

Have we done something similar with the Gospel of the Lord Jesus Christ? Have we just hidden it in our hearts without externalizing it by sharing it with others? Of how many people can we say, "I gave birth to you through the Gospel"?

The Apostle Paul had nothing to reproach himself with on that score. At all times, and in all places, he proclaimed the Gospel in the power of the Holy Spirit; and almost everywhere he went on his missionary journeys he left a nucleus of born-again believers who banded together to form growing Christian communities as local churches.

But, as the spiritual father of the Corinthian Christians, Paul felt an obligation to set before them a good example to follow. Having spoken of his own sacrificial way of living, he doesn't hesitate to ask them to imitate him. He could possibly have been a good teacher without setting a good example. But as their spiritual father he dedicated himself to this life of sacrifice for their sakes, out of love for the Saviour. He could conceivably have lived a so-called Christian life that sought to enjoy all the material amenities of life, in disregard of what that would have meant to God's Kingdom, God's people, and the unbelieving world that he was witnessing to.

But Paul evidently asked himself two questions whenever he had to choose between the permissible and the commendable: First, will it glorify

God by advancing the Gospel? Second, will those who are my spiritual children be encouraged by my example to seek self-satisfaction and self-advancement, or will they be willing to sacrifice for Christ's sake? He knew that what he did never affected only himself but also had an influence on others; that what he did and how he lived spoke louder than what he taught.

The question every servant of God must ask himself is, Can I sincerely and honestly ask the people I led to the Lord through the Gospel to do as I teach and preach, because I'm living up to what I tell them to do? Can I say to my spiritual family, Come to my home and see how I behave Monday through Saturday, or would I prefer that they keep completely out of my private life because of the spiritual inconsistencies with which it is riddled? Though Ecclesiastes 12:11 tells us "the words of the wise are as . . . nails," we would do well to remember that their examples are the hammers that drive them home.

A good example rings louder than any bell to toll people to church. An African prince, after interpreting the missionary's message, said, "I can't read this Book myself," referring to the Bible, "but I believe the words of it because I have watched the missionaries for two years, and they have told me no lies about anything else; so when they tell me this Book is God's Word, I believe it, and I believe that Jesus died for me, and I am going to follow this Jesus."

How many of us could say what Paul did in I Corinthians 4:16: "Wherefore I beseech you, be ye followers of me"? That "wherefore" is important. It is the Greek word *gar,* which could render the meaning here, "This is why I ask you to imitate me." Had Paul not lived the way he did, as described in the previous verses, he could hardly say "therefore follow my example." How do our attitudes in life and service for Christ compare with Paul's? Can we say to newborn babes in Christ, "Therefore imitate me"? Think about it.

Are You an Example for Others?

"Wherefore I beseech you, be ye followers of me" (I Cor. 4:16).

The Life that Wins

A minister was called to the bedside of a dying girl, who had lived for the sinful pleasures of a Christ-rejecting world. The faithful minister did his best to lead her to the Saviour, pleading, praying, and quoting Scripture. Seemingly he could make no impression on her. As a final effort, he called in her mother, who with heartbreaking sorrow also pled with the girl to receive Christ as her Saviour. The girl listened stonily, then said, "Mother, you can't talk to me now. You haven't lived the life before me!"

What a terrible indictment to hear! Those who profess Christ must realize that others are looking to them to be examples worth following. Christ's servant must realize that his spiritual children are ever ready to copy him. When they see him preaching one way and living another, they will be tempted to think, "If he, a supposedly spiritual man, does it, why shouldn't I?" Children often emulate the behavior of their father. A smoker is likely to beget a smoker; a drinker, a drinker; a liar, a liar.

The Apostle Paul realized that those to whom he had given spiritual birth were weaker and less knowledgeable than he, and were therefore ready to copy him. "I have shewed you all things," he wrote to the elders at Ephesus, "how that so labouring ye ought to support the weak" (Acts 20:35). He must always have checked up on himself by asking, Is my weak child in the faith going to become weaker or stronger by observing what I do?

A Salvation Army captain was preaching in Hyde Park in London when a man in the crowd interrupted him. "We haven't anything against Jesus of Nazareth," he said, "but we have something against you Christians because you ain't up to sample." Living examples of Christ is what the world wants to see in Christians.

Primarily what Paul meant by saying, "Therefore be ye followers of me," is that they should follow his example of voluntary suffering for the sake of Jesus Christ. Was there any intrinsic value in such suffering? Not really. But as we look at Romans 8:18 we see how Paul brings out the relationship between the future glory of the believer and the suffering he is willing to undergo for the sake of his Lord. "For I reckon that the sufferings of this present time are not worthy to be compared with the glory which shall be revealed in us," he says. The glory to come will be proportionate to our willingness to endure necessary suffering for Christ here and now. Again, let me stress that suffering in itself, or that we bring upon ourself, is without merit. It is suffering that comes to us as a result of

178

serving Christ that, willingly accepted, is praiseworthy in His sight.

Paul was a gentleman by education and position. For him to take up with a small sect of ignorant fanatics, as the Jewish world held the primitive Christians to be, was the extreme of foolishness so far as material advantages were concerned. Again and again this faithful servant of Christ alludes to this, and so did others. "Paul, thou art beside thyself," said the Roman magistrate; "much learning doth make thee mad" (Acts 26:24). This is what his whole circle of acquaintances outside the Christian community must have thought.

And what a life it was he chose! He says, "What things were gain to me, those I counted loss for Christ. . . . for whom I have suffered the loss of all things, and do count them but refuse, that I may win Christ, and be found in him" (Phil. 3:7-9). Paul longed for every believer to partake of as much of the glory yet to be revealed as possible. But he also knew that this would be in proportion to their sufferings undergone for Christ's sake. That is why he was emboldened to write out of his own experience, "Be ye followers of me."

Paul knew that such a life is really unpopular. Therefore he was careful to attract the Corinthians to it, not by command, but by request. He does not say, "I command you to be followers of me," but "I beseech you." The Greek word translated "beseech" is *parakaloo*, (or *parakale-oo*, as it appears in the lexicons), which literally means "to stand near one and call on him." It is the same word used today in Modern Greek to say "please." It's a polite request, not an order.

What preacher could order his congregation to embrace a life of sacrifice and tears for Christ's sake? One by one his spiritual children would abandon him. He has to set the example first. Even then, the preacher can't force anyone to do as he does and live as he lives. Christ gives the prerogative of choosing a life of suffering over a life of compromise. No one loses his salvation by giving only five percent of his income to the Lord, for instance. But he does lose the joy of obedience to Christ's example. But even if you were so sacrificial as to give fifty percent, you would get nowhere by ordering those around you to follow your example. To win followers to a life of sacrifice, you have to be persuasive and beseeching. Christ Himself proved by His life and death that love is more powerful to win followers than any array of mere physical force or psychological coercion.

Should Christians Imitate Others?

Every dedicated minister of the Gospel knows the heartache and frustration of preaching his heart out to a congregation that listens politely to what he says on Sunday, and then goes about "business as usual" the rest of the week. Sometimes he may be tempted to thunder at them in tones of ringing denunciation in order to awaken them to their responsibilities as Christians. But, if he yields to this impulse, he will only arouse resentment.

If the children of God are to be persuaded to sacrifice for Christ, they must not be coerced but convicted by the Holy Spirit and impelled by Him whose name is the Paraclete, *Parakleetos* in Greek, "the Comforter, the Beseecher," whose name is derived from this same word Paul uses for "beseech," *parakaloo*. Let us not become angry with those who do not do as we do, but let us beseech them through the Holy Spirit. It's no use living in a hut for Christ's sake and complaining all the time that others aren't following our example.

When people see how cheerful and undemanding we are in the state we have chosen to live for Christ's sake, they are more likely to see the advantages of such a life. Let's never say, "Do as I do, or you are no good!" Rather let us say with Paul, "I beseech you" to find out how joyful it is to be fully surrendered to Christ. The joy of personal surrender is the greatest destroyer of the spirit of compromise. Be loving as you call upon others to follow your example. And of course, be very sure that your example is worth following.

How should you express Christianity? In the home, by love and unselfishness. In business, by honesty and diligence. In society, by purity, courtesy, and humility. Toward the unfortunate, by sympathy and mercy. Toward the weak, by helpfulness and patience. Toward the wicked, by overcoming evil without compromise. Toward the strong, by trust and cooperation with good. Toward non-Christians, by witnessing to Christ and His Gospel. Toward the penitent, by forgiveness and restoration. Toward the fortunate, by rejoicing with them without envy. Toward God, by reverence, love, and obedience.

A veteran minister in an address to a group of newly ordained ministers said, "Young men, believe me, you will make more people Christians by being Christians yourselves than you will by all the sermons you will ever preach."

Henry M. Stanley found Livingstone in Africa and lived with him for some time. Here is his testimony: "I went to Africa as prejudiced as the biggest atheist in London. But there came for me a long time for reflection. I saw this solitary old man there and asked myself, 'How on earth does he stop here—is he cracked, or what? What is it that inspires him?'

"For months after we met, I found myself wondering at the old man carrying out all that was said in the Bible—'Leave all things and follow Me.' But little by little his sympathy for others became contagious. My sympathy was aroused, seeing his piety, his gentleness, his zeal, his earnestness, and how he went about his business. I was converted by him, although he had not tried to do it."

Actually, the Apostle Paul was not asking the Corinthian Christians to be his "followers," as the Authorized Version has it in I Corinthians 4:16, but his "imitators." The Greek word is *mimeetai,* which is similar to the Greek word from which we get the English word "mimic." A mimic is one who copies another person's actions. But should even the most consecrated Christian set himself up as a model for others to copy? What about the individuality God means each of us to have? Am I supposed to be what someone else is? Are you? Or am I to expect others to be what I am? Isn't that being somewhat presumptuous and egotistical on the part of the one who says it, and a little unintelligent on the part of those who unthinkingly follow such a course? Who does anyone think he is to suggest that everyone follow him? Why shouldn't people be allowed to express their own individuality? Why encourage them to be mimics? As Louis Albert Banks says, "To be a mere copyist of other people is the most dreary and monotonous outlook that can be presented to any human soul. Nothing cramps and fetters and cripples progress more than that."

One thing Paul did not mean by asking the Corinthians to imitate him was that they should mechanically copy all his actions. As a literal imitation of Christ in all the circumstances of His life (such as being a carpenter, riding a donkey into Jerusalem, chasing the money-changers out of the

182

temple, etc.) was out as far as Paul was concerned, so was his idea of a literal imitation of himself by others.

For instance, Paul chose to remain single, either never having been married, or, as seems more probable, having become a widower. That does not mean that all Christians should remain single. A mechanical imitation of anyone does not demonstrate intelligent appreciation of the spirit but a stupid and slavish conformity to outward appearances. Even if such an imitation were possible, it would be like the mechanical actions of a robot.

No word of Paul's is more penetrating than this: "The letter killeth, but the spirit giveth life" (II Cor. 3:6).

How Can We Imitate God?

In the last section we concluded that slavish imitation of even the best Christians is not what is meant by following their example. When the Apostle Paul wrote to the Corinthian Christians, "Wherefore I beseech you, be ye followers of me," he didn't want to set himself up as some sort of moral or spiritual hero on whom everyone should mechanically pattern his actions. Nor did he consider Christ in that light. To him, Christ was not merely the Jesus of history to be copied, but the Heavenly Visitor who becomes the possessor of our spirits. Only as God the Son indwells us, can we do the acts that He performed when He was here on earth. To live as Christ lived, we must have Christ in us. And, if we are to be imitators of Paul, the Spirit of Christ that prompted him to live as he did must live in us also.

Could I be called a Christian
If everybody knew

My secret thoughts and feelings
  And everything I do?
Oh, could they see the likeness
  Of Christ in me each day?
Oh, could they hear Him speaking
  In every word I say?

Paul's request for the Corinthians to imitate him was based on the assumption that they knew that he was an imitator of Christ. In fact, in I Corinthians 11:1 he states this very clearly, "Be ye followers of me, even as I also am of Christ." If he were not, he would be inexcusably presumptuous in asking others to imitate him. If we are not faithfully following Christ, we have no right to ask others to follow our example.

The fundamental truth, then, is that it is possible for a redeemed human being like Paul to be what Christ is, not merely by mimicking the human Jesus as He lived on earth, but by imitating God. Paul tells us the way to do this in Ephesians 5:1, when he says, "Be ye therefore followers of God, as dear children." That's the only way it can be done. We can only be imitators of God when He is our Father through the new birth, and we are His children. No unregenerated person can imitate God.

This is the only place in Scripture where "imitation" is applied to man's relation to God. Imitation is natural to a child. So it is to the child of God. This indicates that by His indwelling Spirit we have the capacity to act as God acts, to show forth to the world what God is. Of course, we do not acquire full maturity immediately on being born of God. As the child imitates the father at various stages of growth, so we imitate God more faithfully as we grow in our spiritual lives.

God made us for no other end than to be like Him. He didn't make us in the image of any of the heavenly host. Genesis 1:26 tells us, "God said, Let us make man in our image, after our likeness." We lost that image and likeness through sin, which is why Christ had to come to die to redeem us. Through Him God's image and likeness are restored in us, when we receive Him as Saviour and Lord.

Just as a cat cannot imitate a human being, so an unregenerate human being cannot imitate God. It takes a basic correspondence of nature before there can be the possibility of sincere imitation.

But how can we imitate God? In Christ, we have the infinite Father exhibited to us in finite human form, expressing His nature through the life of His Son. Looking at Him, we behold as in a mirror the glories of the invisible God reflected in the person of Jesus Christ; and contemplating these glories we "are changed into the same image from glory to glory even as by the Spirit of God" (II Cor. 3:18).

One of the causes of defective holiness among us is the neglect of the careful study of God's character, as revealed in Christ. We accept the doctrine of justification in the Epistles, but then forget to seek to be like Christ, the perfect Man in the Gospels. No wonder we are so little like Him, if we do not even spend time contemplating His perfections.

It was as their spiritual father that Paul besought the Corinthians to imitate him. Without the filial relationship, imitation of God is impossible. If we are truly His children, there have been implanted in us certain instincts, desires, qualities, and attributes which are in their nature divine; and these will have a tendency to assert themselves in our life and conduct. To yield to those tendencies is to become imitators of God; to check such tendencies—and they may easily be checked—is to neutralize the privileges of our new birth, and to lose the special spiritual benefits that belong to us as children of the Heavenly Father.

How important it is, then, that in our personal experience we should watch over all within us that seems to come from God. These holy aspirations and purer instincts of which we are conscious have been introduced to our nature by divine grace; they come not of earth; they have their home in the very heart of God Himself.

How to Follow Paul's Example

Someone has observed that the acid test of anyone's dedication to a cause is his pocketbook. It reminds me of the Quaker who met an acquaintance on the street. In the course of conversation, the name of a poor family came up. "I really feel for them," said the second man. "How does thee feel for them, friend?" asked the Quaker. "With thy pocket?"

It's often difficult for those who are well off to understand how anyone would voluntarily accept a life of poverty. Probably the Corinthian Christians in their affluent state felt a bit contemptuous of the Apostle Paul for choosing a life of privation. By telling them they ought to imitate him, even as he had imitated Christ—since they were his spiritual children—he was telling them they needed to strengthen their filial instincts and develop them into habits of life.

Children ought to want to be like their father. A little child naturally thinks his father the greatest man in the world—that is, if he is worthy of the name father. That's the attitude the Corinthians should have entertained for Paul, who had labored so lovingly and untiringly among them to exemplify Christ, and to lead them to experience the new birth. As natural sonship prompts an admiration that leads the child to attempt an imitation of what the father does, however feebly, so the Corinthians should have felt that way toward Paul, whose spiritual children they were. A true imitation begins within, in the condition of the spirit, rather than outwardly, in conduct; though the lessons that the inner spirit learns will surely express themselves in outward actions.

What Paul meant by saying "Be ye imitators of me" was not that the Corinthians should slavishly follow everything he did in minutest detail. The application to ourselves, therefore, is not that we should thoughtlessly do what Paul did, with careless disregard of the circumstances and the needs of the times, as well as the cultural and family setting in which each of us is found.

I have spoken previously of Paul's choice to remain single, either as a widower or as never having been married. Although we have no clear indication of his marital status, it seems likely that he was a widower, since he was a member of the Sanhedrin before he became a Christian, and all members of this Jewish high court had to be married.

Paul preferred to stay unmarried, but he did not insist that others should imitate him in this. "If thou marry, thou hast not sinned," he said in I Corinthians 7:28, "and if a virgin marry, she hath not sinned." In fact, he wrote of marriage in general, "I will therefore that the younger women marry, bear children, guide the house, give none occasion to the adversary to speak reproachfully" (I Tim. 5:14). And again, in I Timothy 3:12, he said, "Let the deacons be the husbands of one wife, ruling their children and their own houses well."

What did Paul mean, then, when he requested us to follow his example? Not necessarily to stay single simply because he chose to. That was his own choice as a means to accomplish an end that he believed God had set in his life—to make Christ known to the far corners of the then-known world.

It is attitudes that count in our Christian lives. Staying single or getting married is not significant in itself and has no merit either way. The question to ask when making such a decision is, In view of what God has called me to accomplish in life, how can I best accomplish it—by being married or staying single?

And there are other considerations to take into account. What impression will I leave on others? Will my staying single encourage others blindly to follow me, to the detriment of their own lives and the cause of Christ? When we have considered all things, then we should decide on the merits of the case as they affect God's work, others, and last of all our personal comfort, pleasure, and idiosyncrasies.

Take another instance of Paul's attitudes in his service for Christ, that of being paid for his ministry. He preferred not to be paid for preaching and pastoring, but to support himself by his trade of tent-making. When he desired to go to Corinth from Athens, he didn't have to wait until he "raised" enough support, as so many missionaries do. Instead he was able to go there fully depending upon his profitable trade. That was also the case with his co-workers and hosts in Corinth, Priscilla and Aquila; they, too, were self-supporting (Acts 18:3).

Had Paul been other than self-supporting, he might never have traveled to Corinth to bring the Gospel to some half-million people who lived in heathen darkness. I wonder whether Paul would have refused an offering had it been forthcoming. I doubt it. The main purpose of his life at that time was to carry the Gospel to Corinth by all means—

whether by tent-making and thus preaching only part time, or by receiving support from God's people and giving his full time to the ministry. The goal is the important thing, not the means—either of which would have been legitimate in this case.

Should Preachers Demand Their Rights?

The Apostle Paul was very careful not to bring the Gospel into disrepute by any action or attitude of his. That's why he labored with his own hands to support himself in the ministry. With what satisfaction he must have said to the Ephesians, "Yea, ye yourselves know, that these hands have ministered unto my necessities, and to them that were with me. I have shewed you all things, how that so labouring ye ought to support the weak, and to remember the words of the Lord Jesus, how he said, It is more blessed to give than to receive" (Acts 20:34,35).

Did Paul demand a free parsonage? No. In Rome, when he was taken there as a prisoner, he hired his own house. That was toward the end of his life. Couldn't all the people he had evangelized, and especially the well-to-do Corinthian Christians, have contributed to the rent of that house? It is to their shame that they didn't. But Paul may have preferred to pay the rent himself.

In Acts 28:30 we read, "And Paul dwelt two whole years in his own hired house, and received all that came in unto him." I can imagine how he must have felt as he wrote to the Corinthian Christians, "Now ye are full, now ye are rich, ye have reigned as kings without us." And then he contrasts the fate of the apostles: "appointed to death: for we are made a spectacle unto the world. . . . Even unto this present hour we both hunger, and thirst, and are naked, and are buffeted, and have no certain dwellingplace" (I Cor. 4:8-11).

189

Think of Paul, that self-sacrificing servant of God who had evangelized thousands, at the very end of his life waiting to die in Rome at the hands of his persecutors, having to pay his own rent! Pastor, teacher, parent, do you sometimes feel neglected by those to whom you ministered in the past, or are still ministering? Think of Paul in his hired house in Rome paying his own rent from the proceeds of his past tent-making. And then listen to him say, "Be ye imitators of me." I'm sure he would have accepted a rental allowance or a prison parsonage had it been offered to him, but apparently it had not. Nevertheless, he did not give up the goal set before him, to preach the Gospel in Rome also.

What is the example we are to follow, in the light of Paul's words and actions? Not necessarily that we must have a secular job or pay our own rent if we are ministers of the Gospel. But if those we minister to as a pastor or missionary refuse to support us, and do not provide a rent-free home, we do not give up preaching and making God's grace known. Paul didn't want us to follow the less excellent way of giving God only part of our time; but, if it had to be that way, he felt that part-time ministry was better than none.

Paul was very sensitive about possible criticism of his actions that could adversely affect the Gospel. He took the times, the people, and the circumstances into account when making his decisions. Decisions ought not to be made in a vacuum. We must ask ourselves not only about the rightness or wrongness of our acts, but also about how they will affect God's work, our fellow believers, and those whom we are seeking to win to Christ.

What Paul did in certain circumstances may not be what God wants you and me to do in our own particular circumstances. Our situations may vary widely from Paul's but we must learn to surrender our rights for the Gospel's sake. This does not mean we must concede that they are not our rights; we simply relinquish them freely out of a desire to serve Christ whatever the cost. God pity anyone who gives up ministering simply because his rights cannot be satisfied.

Listen to Paul speak about the rights of ministers: "Even so hath the Lord ordained that they which preach the gospel should live of the gospel. But I have used none of these things: neither have I written these things, that it should be so done unto me: for it were better for me to die, than that any man should make my glorying void. For though I preach the gospel, I have nothing to glory of: for necessity is laid upon me; yea, woe is unto me, if I preach not the gospel! For if I do this thing willingly, I have a reward: but if against my will, a dispensation of the gospel is committed unto me. What is my reward then? Verily that, when I preach the gospel, I may make the gospel of Christ without charge, that I abuse not my power in the gospel" (I Cor. 9:14-18).

Thus, in saying "Be ye imitators of me," Paul doesn't necessarily mean his actions but his attitudes and philosophy of life—always taking into consideration the circumstances and culture of the time and the need of the hour. Never allow the attitudes of others to hinder you from doing what you believe to be your God-appointed task.

Let us follow Paul's example in that, while we do our task—and others are not doing their duty toward us—we do not become bitter toward them. Consider with what sweetness Paul wrote to the Thessalonians, "For ye remember, brethren, our labour and travail: for labouring night and day, because we would not be chargeable unto any of

you, we preached unto you the gospel of God"
(I Thess. 2:9).

No Instant Perfection

We have seen in our study of the life of the
Apostle Paul that he voluntarily accepted a life of
hardship, even to the extent of earning his living by
tent-making, so that he could preach the Gospel
without charge. Does that mean that Paul refused
help from those he ministered to? No, for we are
told that at Melita he was showered with many gifts.
In Acts 28:10 we read that the people of Melita
"also honoured us with many honours; and when
we departed, they laded us with such things as were
necessary." Also the Philippians must have contributed to Paul's needs, as he expressed his gratitude to them in Philippians 4:10: "But I rejoiced in
the Lord greatly, that now at the last your care of me
hath flourished again; wherein ye were also careful,
but ye lacked opportunity."

And then, in verses 15-18 he adds: "Now ye
Philippians know also, that in the beginning of the
gospel, when I departed from Macedonia, no church
communicated with me as concerning giving and
receiving, but ye only. For even in Thessalonica ye
sent once and again unto my necessity. Not because
I desire a gift: but I desire fruit that may abound to
your account. But I have all, and abound: I am full,
having received from Epaphroditus the things which
were sent from you, an odour of a sweet smell, a
sacrifice acceptable, well-pleasing to God."

The verb Paul uses in the clause "be ye
followers of me" in I Corinthians 4:16 is *ginesthe,*
which is the present imperative of *ginomai,* meaning
"to become." Paul is not calling Christians to a state
of being they can attain by a single act. He is not
beseeching the Corinthians to do something that

will instantly make his choices theirs. Their imitation of Paul was to be gradual. They were to grow into the measure of his stature in Christ.

This was a little different from the imitating he spoke of in I Thessalonians 1:6 and 2:14. In these verses he used the aorist tense of the verb *ginomai* to express their instantaneous and once-and-for-all following of his example in accepting the word of truth unto salvation. "And ye became *[egeneetheete]* our imitators, and of the Lord, having received *[dexamenoi,* the aorist participle] the word in much affliction, with joy of the Holy Spirit." As Paul had received the word of salvation once and for all and instantly, so did they. That is regeneration, our entrance into the Kingdom of God.

But then comes the constant imitating of Paul's life. We need to examine his attitudes and philosophy with an eye to the principle involved. His own comfort and worldly glory never came first; it was always what was best for God's work, even if it meant suffering and privation. As we decide to go without one thing, we will find it easier to go without another. We do not generally reach a life that is fully satisfied by the indwelling presence of Christ in an instant. It is a gradual process. As we face the circumstances of life one by one as Paul would have, as Christ would have, we discover that we gradually are conforming to the characters of these personalities.

There are stages of life in each of which we can show our perfection in Christ. Take a six-month-old baby; we don't expect him to act as a six-year-old should. But we would be disturbed if after five years he still acted like a six-month-old. Growth is necessary; and that was Paul's burden for the Corinthians. They were saved but they were not growing spiritually. "Therefore be ye imitators of me" meant "Keep growing in grace. Keep getting more and more mature. Don't attempt to reach the height of God's expectation for you by a boisterous and instant act.''

So many of us are like that gourd that wound itself around a lofty palm tree, and in a few weeks climbed to the very top. "How old are you?" asked the newcomer. "About one hundred years," said the palm. "About one hundred years, and no taller?!! Only look, I have grown as tall as you in fewer days than you count years." "I know that well," replied the palm. "Every summer of my life a gourd has climbed up around me as proud as you are, and as short-lived as you will be."

Paul didn't want the Corinthians to be like spiritual gourds whose climb was fast but short-lived. The moment we reach the conclusion that we have attained our full growth as Christians, that is the moment we need to re-evaluate our lives to see where we really are. We need to go over Paul's experiences for Christ's sake, enumerated in I Corinthians 4:9-13, and ask ourselves whether in each of them we have become his imitators. We may not have had to make the same choices he did, but if it came right down to it, would we be willing to? It's a soul-searching question.

Compromise or Sacrifice—the Acid Test of Faith

If the Apostle Paul were writing to your church or mine today, I wonder if he could say what he wrote to the Thessalonian church in his day. "For ye, brethren, became [*egeneethete,* in the aorist tense] followers [imitators] of the churches of God which in Judea are in Christ Jesus: for ye also have suffered [*epathete,* aorist] like things of your own countrymen, even as they have of the Jews" (I Thess. 2:14).

Paul wrote these words to a church that in a particular instance imitated another church that suffered for the sake of Christ. Just as one gets used to compromise and is no longer deeply distressed by it, so it is with suffering as a consequence of faithfulness; it becomes second nature. The important question is, are we moving toward the pull of our carnal nature in compromising with the world, or toward conformity to Christ and Paul in resisting evil and suffering privation so that Christ may be glorified?

So many of us think of compromise only in theological matters and the common practices of the world in which Christians might feel tempted to participate. But Paul here intimates a compromise that few of us like to think about. It is keeping up with the Joneses! It is spending our time and money acquiring things we don't really need but which would enhance our social status and fame.

The converse of this is choosing to live modestly or even sacrificially when we could live it up for the glory of self. When we quit the Lord's work just for the sake of an easier life, that's compromise. The Apostolic way may not be as easy, or provide us with all the comforts of the world, but it's the Christlike, the Paul-like way.

Moses, in his day, had to make such a choice. We read in Hebrews 11:24, 25: "By faith Moses, when he was come to years, refused to become the son of Pharaoh's daughter; choosing rather to suffer affliction with the people of God, than to enjoy the pleasures of sin for a season." Moses' choice represents one of the most extraordinary and deliberate acts of renunciation of worldly advantage in favor of spiritual values that the world has ever known.

And why did he do it? Why did he give up the palace, with all its luxuries, pleasures, and privileges, and identify himself with the downtrodden children of Israel? What was his reward for incurring Pharaoh's displeasure and enmity? Hebrews 11:26 goes on to tell us his motive: "Esteeming the reproach of Christ greater riches than the treasures in Egypt: for he had respect unto the recompence of the reward." He was influenced in his choice by the promise God had given to Israel of a coming Messiah.

His reward by worldly standards was hardly one to be envied. His life was fraught with peril as he braved the wrath of Pharaoh in pronouncing God's plagues on Egypt. It was no easy task he had organizing the Israelites into a faith-filled and cooperative marching band as they fled toward the Red Sea. And his forty-year endurance contest in the wilderness, leading an often discouraged and rebellious people, would surely seem a poor exchange for the pleasures of Egypt. What was his secret? Hebrews 11:27 tells us, "He endured, as seeing him who is invisible."

Moses and the Apostle Paul were cast in the same self-sacrificing mold, for the sake of Christ. And we who strive to follow in their footsteps must be willing to make the same hard choices when the cause of Christ requires them of us. John Newton knew something of this when he wrote:

> I asked the Lord that I might grow
>   In faith and love and every grace;
> Might more of His salvation know
>   And seek more earnestly His face.
>
> 'Twas He who taught me thus to pray,
>   And He, I know, has answered prayer;
> But it has been in such a way
>   As almost drove me to despair.

196

I hoped that in some favored hour
 At once He'd answer my request,
And by His love's constraining power
 Subdue my sins, and give me rest.

Instead of this, He made me feel
 The hidden evils of my heart,
And let the angry powers of Hell
 Assault my soul in every part.

Yea! more; with His own hand He seemed
 Intent to aggravate my woe;
Crossed all the fair designs I schemed,
 Blasted my gourds, and laid me low.

"Lord, why is this?" I trembling cried.
 "Wilt Thou pursue Thy worm to death?"
"'Tis in this way," the Lord replied,
 "I answer prayer for grace and faith.

"These inward trials I employ
 From self and pride to set Thee free,
And break thy schemes of earthly joy,
 That thou mayest seek thy All in Me."

Timothy's Role as
Paul's Delegate to Corinth

"For this cause have I sent unto you Timotheus, who is my beloved son, and faithful in the Lord, who shall bring you into remembrance of my ways which be in Christ, as I teach every where in every church" (I Cor. 4:17).

Don't Be a "Feudamentalist"

Before Paul sent his First Epistle to the Corinthians, he prepared the way for it by sending Timothy to Corinth. I Corinthians 4:17 is made clearer to us by paraphrasing what he had said as follows: "Not only am I writing to you to tell you of my conduct as an apostle, but I have also sent you my spiritual son, Timothy, to tell you all about it." According to I Corinthians 16:10, Timothy must have arrived in Corinth after Paul's letter (I Corinthians) got there. So first they were told of Paul's attitudes through this letter, then by the mouth of Timothy, and then Paul intended to follow up Timothy's visit with one of his own, which may or may not have taken place.

Thus Timothy left Ephesus for Corinth to convey Paul's message in person. He wanted Timothy to bring them an explanation of his attitudes in general, to prepare them more or less for the receipt of his letter to follow with more explicit information concerning his apostolic ways. Why did he choose Timothy for this particular mission? Who was Timothy?

His name meant "to honor God," and was derived from the Greek verb *timaoo,* "to honor," and *Theos,* "God." He was the son of a mixed marriage. His mother was a Jewess and his father was a Greek (Acts 16:1). It was his mother Eunice and his maternal grandmother Lois who taught him the Scriptures from an early age (II Tim. 1:5). He was a native of Lystra, in Asia Minor. The fact that Paul calls him his child in the Lord in I Corinthians 4:17 suggests that he was actually converted to Christ through Paul's ministry in Lystra. In spite of the fact of his godly upbringing by his mother and grandmother, he needed to come to the point of personal acceptance of Jesus Christ.

When Paul wrote his first letter to Timothy as a pastor, he called him "my own son in the faith" (I Tim. 1:2). He took an affectionately paternal attitude toward him. And he maintains the same attitude toward the Corinthian Christians as he had maintained all along toward Timothy—that of a spiritual father. That is the sweetest attitude one could have toward anybody. Thus Paul sent one spiritual child of his to encourage and admonish his fellow children in Corinth.

The sense of brotherhood in the Christian Church is one of the greatest cohesive powers in the world. Paul wanted Timothy to go, not as a teacher with an attitude of superiority, an air of "Do as I tell you or else," but as a fellow child of Paul and a brother in Christ. The bond of having Paul in common as their spiritual father was an important consideration in making Timothy Paul's corrective emissary. The Apostle felt that the Corinthians ought to listen to Timothy if for no other reason, at least, than that he was his son in the Lord, just as they were his spiritual sons, as he pointed out to them in I Corinthians 1:16.

Another reason Paul may have chosen Timothy to go to Corinth was that his father was a Greek and presumably a pagan. He was the product of a mixed marriage, a common thing in Corinth, as we see from the 7th chapter of this epistle. It was therefore easier for him to understand the problems of homes with mixed marriages, where the children were perplexed by the duties they owed to the Lord and those they owed to their parents.

As the son of a Greek father, Timothy would also have been well acquainted with the tendency of the Greek mind to make *a priori* philosophical judgments, such as the biological impossibility of the resurrection of the body. If you will read I Corinthians 15, and study my 860-page exposition of it in *Conquering the Fear of Death,* you will see how methodically and pragmatically Paul proves that facts—such as the historically authenticated resurrection of the body of Jesus—negate any such philosophical speculations. His thesis is, here are the proofs; it happened; Christ arose. Therefore the resurrection of the human body is not only possible, but it will most certainly occur.

Furthermore, Timothy was a living demonstration of Paul's attitude toward certain matters he deemed not essential to the Christian faith, such as circumcision. As the child of a Jewess and a Greek, Timothy had not been circumcised as the Jewish law prescribed. Apparently this aroused opposition to Timothy and Paul among Christians of Jewish background as well as among unbelieving Jews.

Although Paul stood for the principle of not subjecting Gentile Christians to the Jewish ceremonial laws, he decided to circumcise Timothy so that the ministry among the Jews might not be hindered. "Paul . . . took and circumcised him because of the Jews which were in those quarters: for they knew all that his father was a Greek" (Acts 16:3).

This was not compromise but an example of how a Christian should act in similar circumstances. This philosophy is predominant in all Paul's teaching, as seen also in Romans 14, where he says that, if by eating or not eating certain foods he might offend others, he would accommodate himself to their customs. Timothy was a living example of Paul's attitude. He could say to the feuding Corinthians, We must learn to respect the culture of others if that does not entail the abandonment of fundamental principles. The failure to distinguish between what is fundamental and what is trivial makes "feudamentalists."

Trying to Remedy a Bad Situation in the Church

In the previous section we were talking about Timothy, Paul's son in the faith, whom he sent to the Corinthians to share with them the things that were on Paul's heart concerning their spiritual welfare.

In Acts 16:3 we read that Paul, Silas, and Timothy traveled westward toward the Aegean Coast of Asia Minor. Nothing more is recorded of Timothy in the Acts until they reached Berea (Acts 17:14). There they agreed that Paul would go on to Athens, leaving Silas and Timothy behind. From Athens, Paul went on to Corinth, where Silas and Timothy later joined him (Acts 18:5). This was not the visit referred to by Paul in I Corinthians 4:17. It was a later visit. Thus we see that Timothy was no stranger to the Corinthians, as he had been there with Paul and Silas (II Cor. 1:19).

The next we hear of Timothy, he was in Ephesus with Paul, and was sent from there to Macedonia, along with Erastus (Acts 19:22). It was from there that he proceeded to Corinth on the occasion referred to by Paul in I Corinthians 4:17.

Apparently Timothy was of a retiring nature, for Paul urges the Corinthians to set him at ease and not to despise him. "Now if Timotheus come, see that he may be with you without fear: for he worketh the work of the Lord, as I also do. Let no man therefore despise him: but conduct him forth in peace, that he may come unto me: for I look for him with the brethren" (I Cor. 16:10, 11).

From the situation that developed in Corinth, it is evident that Timothy's mission was not successful, and it is significant that though Timothy's name is associated with Paul's in the greeting in II Corinthians 1:1, it is Titus and not Timothy who has become the apostolic delegate. (See II Cor. 7:6, 13, 14; 8:6, 16, 23; 12:18).

Between the time Paul sent Timothy to Corinth to make his ways known to them and the time he wrote his first epistle to them, he had received news about their situation from Chloe's people, who came from Corinth to see him at Ephesus. Thus in I Corinthians 1:11 we read, "For it hath been declared unto me of you, my brethren, by them which are of the house of Chloe, that there are contentions among you."

News also came to Paul about conditions in Corinth from Stephanas, Fortunatus, and Achaicus, as we see in I Corinthians 16:17. These three had apparently gone from Ephesus to Corinth, and back to Ephesus, to bring the news to Paul. And in the meantime Paul must have received a letter from the Corinthians asking his advice on several perplexing problems. It was probably in answer to this information from individuals and their letter that Paul wrote to them about certain specific matters.

Thus in I Corinthians 7:1 he wrote, "Now concerning the things whereof ye wrote unto me. . . ." And he goes on to give answers to their questions. This letter must have arrived in Corinth before Timothy got there. Paul wanted it to prepare the Corinthians to give Timothy a good reception. That's why he said in I Corinthians 16:10, "Now if Timotheus come, see that he may be with you without fear: for he worketh the work of the Lord, as I also do."

Paul fully intended to follow up Timothy's visit to Corinth by his personal presence, as we see in Acts 19:21, 22: "After these things were ended [in Ephesus, from which he wrote the Corinthian epistles], Paul purposed in the spirit, when he had passed through Macedonia and Achaia [of which Corinth was the principal city], saying, After I have been there, I must also see Rome. So he sent into Macedonia two of them that ministered unto him, Timotheus and Erastus; but he himself stayed in Asia [that's Ephesus and its environment] for a season."

Whether Paul was able to pay a second visit to Corinth, as he expressed a desire to in I Corinthians 4:19, is not clearly stated in the record. "But I will come to you shortly, if the Lord will . . . ." However, since he speaks of coming to the Corinthians for the third time, in II Corinthians 12:14 and 13:1, 2, we can safely assume that the second visit spoken of in Acts 19:21 and I Corinthians 4:19 must have taken place. Unfortunately, we only have the record of Paul's first visit to Corinth, and that briefly, in Acts

18:1-17. Of the second and third visits we have no record as to his teaching and ministry among them. Corinth from Ephesus was about two or three days by boat. Both were important port cities joined by ships.

Despite Paul's first letter to the Corinthians in answer to theirs, and the sending of Timotheus, followed by his second and third visits among them, apparently the troubled situation in the church of Corinth did not get any better. Paul consequently had to write a very stern letter to them, which we shall take up in our next study.

Situational Ethics Versus Moral Absolutes

As a parent, what do you do when kindness and reasoning fail to bring about a change of conduct in a rebellious child? You adopt sterner measures, right? And that's what the Apostle Paul had to do when his first epistle to the Corinthians, and the sending of his spiritual son Timothy, failed to correct the disturbing situation in their church.

In II Corinthians 2:4 we read, "For out of much affliction and anguish of heart I wrote unto you with many tears; not that ye should be grieved, but that ye might know the love which I have more abundantly unto you." And then in chapter 7, verse 8, he wrote, "For though I made you sorry with a letter, I do not repent, though I did repent [i.e., changed my mind]: for I perceive that the same epistle has made you sorry, though it were but for a season."

The letter referred to here apparently was so severe that Paul was sorry he had ever sent it. Where is this letter? Most probably it is what we have in II Corinthians 10 to 13. These four chapters, then, should actually precede chapters 1 to 9 of II Corinthians. This sternly worded letter contained in chapters 10 to 13 was sent by Titus. (See II Cor. 2:13 and 7:13.) Apparently this letter, and Titus, were more successful in setting things in order in Corinth.

After learning of the improved situation, Paul wrote what may be considered as the Third Epistle to the Corinthians, actually contained in II Corinthians 1 through 9. He wrote of Titus' visit among them in II Corinthians 7:13, "Therefore we were comforted in your comfort: yea, and exceedingly the more joyed we for the joy of Titus, because his spirit was refreshed by you all." Then, after Titus' visit and the wonderful results of his second epistle, he wrote his letter of reconciliation contained in II Corinthians 1-9. Read chapters 10-13 first, and then chapters 1-9, and you will see that the sequence makes sense.

One more question, and that is, where do we find the letter that apparently preceded I Corinthians? In I Corinthians 5:9 Paul says, "I wrote unto you in an epistle not to company with fornicators." Where is this epistle? It may have been lost. However, some scholars believe that it's what we have in II Corinthians 6:14—7:1. Its contents fit the subject mentioned in I Corinthians 5:9. As you come to II Corinthians 6:13, skip to II Corinthians 7:2 and see how naturally they connect.

Let's not forget that the words of Scripture are inspired, but the divisions into chapters are the work of men in the 13th century and the divisions into verses took place in the 16th century.

Here, then, is the probable order in which the Corinthian epistles should be read:

1) II Corinthians 6:14—7:1
2) I Corinthians
3) II Corinthians 10-13
4) II Corinthians 1:1—6:13; 7:2—9:15

As we study I Corinthians 4:17, we see Paul's method of dealing with the immediate problems of a local Christian congregation. He sends a letter to them after having received personal information about their problems through informants and their own letter. He sends Timothy as his emissary, who arrives after the letter. He would have liked to go himself, but he couldn't. He knew that if he were to accomplish his task he would have to use others to help him.

In all these things, he is an example for us to follow. When we cannot attend to a thing personally, we should use associates who are beloved and faithful. Never mind if they cannot do all that we can. Never mind if those to whom we send them do not welcome them as they would us. We must put first things first, and establish right priorities as far as the apportionment of our time is concerned.

Paul was not in any way abdicating his responsibilities to the Corinthians. He was still dealing with them. He sent Timothy because he had no time to go himself. Observe, however, why he sent him: To "bring you into remembrance of my ways which be in Christ." This implies that they were already aware of Paul's way, but Timothy was sent to remind them of Paul's attitudes and add his own testimony that there was no change. It was not Timothy's responsibility to introduce his own personal opinions among them. He was willing to play a subservient role out of loving obedience to and respect for his spiritual father.

Paul reminded the Corinthians that what he said to them was what he taught in all the churches. He didn't want them to feel they were being treated differently, but he firmly believed that truth should not be accommodated to individual preferences. He was no advocate of situational ethics where absolute moral principles were concerned, but believed truth should be absolute for all. The Corinthians wanted him to sanction a different kind of Christianity among them, one that allowed worldly and immoral practices. Aren't there Christians like that today? Paul wanted them—and us—to know that Christian principles cannot be compromised at will.

How to Know God's Will and Do It

"Now some are puffed up, as though I would not come to you. But I will come to you shortly, if the Lord will, and will know, not the speech of them which are puffed up, but the power" (I Cor. 4:18, 19).

Man's Will Versus God's Will

Arrogance is an unbecoming trait in anyone, but especially so in Christians. In writing to the Corinthian church, Paul foresaw what their reaction would be to his sending Timothy to deal with their problems, instead of coming himself. "Now some of you are puffed up, as though I would not come to you" (I Cor. 4:18). Paul knew their pride would be hurt because of their sense of self-importance, which led them to feel they deserved his personal presence among them. "We deserve the number one man, not the second-in-command" was their attitude.

How many churches are like that! They will not even consider calling a pastor who is not nationally known. There may be a true saint of God available, whose message and ability are Christlike and Spirit filled, but he may lack the fame to satisfy the pride of the Pulpit Committee. They may not want to consider anyone unless he has a Ph.D. and a national reputation.

There was a church once whose choice lay between two seemingly acceptable candidates for the pulpit. But one had a scar on his face, and the other was smooth-cheeked and handsome. They chose the latter; and when his ministry proved weak and ineffectual, a wise old deacon said, "Well, they got what they wanted; a pretty minister; but 'the Lord taketh not pleasure in the legs of a man' " (Ps. 147:10).

Pride was the fundamental sin of the Corinthians. They believed that they ranked first among all Christians and therefore deserved to be ministered to by no one less than Paul himself. They remind me of that sophisticated lady in the Orient who attended a dinner given by a high-ranking British official. The general's assistant seated her at the left of her host rather than at his right. She fumed inwardly until she could no longer bear it. Haughtily she said, "I suppose you have great difficulty getting your aide-de-camp to seat your guests properly." "Not really," said the general. "Those who matter don't mind, and those who mind don't matter."

Some of the Corinthians misunderstood Paul's not coming to Corinth at the time they thought he should. They thought to themselves, "You see, he didn't have the courage to face us himself, so he sent us a letter and then this inexperienced young fellow Timothy, who is not even an apostle. I guess we've won our case. If he were right and we were wrong, he wouldn't have hesitated to come running. Evidently what's happening among us isn't very serious, then." Such reasoning led them to become puffed up, arrogant, proud.

"As though I would not come to you"—that's how the verse begins in Greek. And that forms the basis of their reaction, expressed in the verb *ephusiootheesan,* "puffed up." Paul's thought could be paraphrased as "Some, not all, were puffed up on the presumption that I was not coming to you at all." The verb *phusio-oo,* which is a later substitute for *phusaoo,* is largely limited to Christian literature, and means "to blow up, to puff up." Observe that it was not all who felt that way; not all believed that Paul's failure to come was a sign of weakness.

For the sake of those few who became proud because he didn't visit Corinth, he decided to go, and he tells them so in verse 19: "But I will come to you shortly, if the Lord will, and will know, not the speech of them which are puffed up, but the power." Paul first expressed his determination to go to them quickly; that was the expression of his own will. But he is immediately arrested by a consideration of that greater will, the will of the Lord in his life. And so he adds, "if the Lord will."

There was also a third "will" involved here, the will of the Corinthians. Look at verse 21: "What will ye?" His will, God's will, the wills of the Corinthians. . . . Stop and think. Those are the determinant factors of life.

Although Paul appeared to be putting his will first, "I will come to you shortly," he really placed God's will first. He knew that his will to go was completely subject to God's directive will. The Lord could have made it impossible for him to go in any number of ways. God's will, therefore, must be the Christian's first consideration. The spirit and its will as well as thoughts are the center of man's being. My will is the expression of my character. So God's will is really the expression of God Himself—what God chooses, what God prefers, what God eternally

211

purposes. All man's relationships to God are determined by the relation of God's will to man's will.

Paul's first question when confronted by Christ on the road to Damascus was, "Who art thou?" As soon as he learned it was the Lord, his next question was, "What wilt thou?"—and that was the question he asked for the rest of his life. From that moment he surrendered himself to the mastership of Jesus Christ, and henceforth he knew no other master. He could sing with the hymnwriter: "I own no other Master; my heart shall be Thy throne. My life I give henceforth to live, O Christ, for Thee alone."

The Joy of a Yielded Will

Suppose you were to go into an automotive factory and stand before some great piece of machinery. As you stood there, a small wheel, no bigger than a quarter, came loose and fell into the midst of the machinery. That great mechanism moving round and round would grind that little wheel into fragments.

The universe is one great machine, so to speak, and God is its motive power; and when because of sin a soul drops out of its place in this great machine and falls among the great wheels of God's purpose, it is ground into powder, unless the grace of God puts that wheel back in its place in the machinery.

The moment you find out what the will of God is for you, and drop into your place, all the universe moves with you, and all the universe moves for you. The whole Godhead is back of you—the wisdom of God, the power of God, the love of God, and the grace of God—and you are as absolutely sure and safe as God is. Peter says, "And who is he that will harm you, if ye be followers of that which is good?"

(I Pet. 3:13). To obey the will of the Lord is the secret of all safety and security. And Romans 8:28 says, "We know that all things work together for good to them that love God, to them who are the called according to his purpose."

When we take God's will as ours, we do not destroy ours. There is no war between the two wills, no resentment that ours has been put in harmony with God's. The Apostle Paul knew that if God willed that he not go to Corinth, that would have been his will too. Submitting to God's will is not only safe but it is also the secret of peace and serenity.

President Lincoln was once told by an associate, "I am very anxious that the Lord should be on our side." "Oh," said Mr. Lincoln, "that does not give me the least trouble in the world, sir. The only question is whether we are on the Lord's side. If we are on the Lord's side, we are perfectly safe." It was that kind of faith that made Stephen, the first martyr, smile, and his face light up like the face of an angel, when he was on trial for his life before the council at Jerusalem.

When you yield your will to God you do not destroy your will. You put your will into harmony with His. You open your heart to His leading, and your life becomes the channel through which God flows and pours all the stream of His almighty power. Let it be the prayer of your life to go as you are led, when you are led, where you are led.

When Paul wrote the Corinthians that he was coming to them if the Lord willed, he was declaring that the Lord would gradually and eventually disclose that will to him. Because he saw the need, he wanted to go quickly. But just how quickly, only circumstances determined by God's will would gradually reveal.

We, too, must be willing to await the gradual disclosing of God's will. He doesn't always disclose it immediately. It is very much like that sheet that Peter saw coming down from heaven, in his vision on the housetop. It came down at the hour of prayer, and it ascended again when the hour of prayer was over, and all it revealed to Peter was his immediate duty. "While Peter thought on the vision, the Spirit said unto him, Behold, three men seek thee. Arise therefore, and get thee down, and go with them, doubting nothing; for I have sent them" (Acts 10:19, 20). That vision didn't tell Peter what his duty was next month or next year, but what his duty was just then and there.

Any work in which we are engaged that causes us a great deal of anxiety and fret and sleepless nights is probably not God's work at all. It is something we are doing because of our ambition, our appetite, our greed, our selfishness, or our desire to get on in the world. For if it were God's work we were doing, and we were just putting our hands to God's work, why should we worry about it? Isn't that a kind of impertinence? Isn't God able to take care of His own work? The man on the battlefield who has supreme confidence in the commanding officer and follows him into the thick of the fight doesn't consider himself responsible for the issues of the battle. He knows that there is a competent hand regulating the whole matter, and all he has to do as a soldier is to follow where his leader goes, and strictly to obey his commands.

It is God's will that I should cast
 All care on Him each day;
He also bids me not to cast
 My confidence away.

214

My soul, what folly then is thine,
   When taken unawares,
To cast away thy confidence,
   And carry all thy cares!

—Author Unknown

Guidelines for Determining God's Will

Does following God's will always lead to success? It all depends on what we mean by success. As Christians, we should never equate success with the world's expectations. What the world counts as success, God may call failure; and what man considers failure, God may count as success.

For instance, when Stephen, newly consecrated to the work of God, and just beginning to make headway in his ministry and witness, fell under the rocks hurled at him by his enemies, most men might have said, "What a sad failure, to have his life cut off at the very beginning!"

But there was a young man standing by, looking at that face radiant with God's inner light, on whom it made an indelible impression. He was Saul of Tarsus, and it is very possible that the beginning of his conversion could be traced back to the impressions implanted in his mind when he looked upon the first of the martyrs for Christ. Was Stephen's death an indication that his life had ended in failure? For all we know, Stephen may have died to give the Church Saul of Tarsus as Paul, the apostle to the Gentiles.

When Paul and Silas journeyed to Philippi, a city of Macedonia, in answer to a vision God gave them in the night, and were thrown into prison, with their feet made fast in the stocks, most people might have thought, "Well, their mission certainly is a failure. They must have mistaken their calling." But when at midnight Paul and Silas were singing God's praises, and God answered by an earthquake that shook the prison and released every man's bands, what was the result? The jailer and his family became the firstfruits to Christ of that midnight hour, and what man counted failure, God in heaven counted success.

And when Paul went to Rome and was chained to a soldier of the Praetorian guard, and when every morning a new soldier was chained to him, until the whole Praetorian guard had had Paul under custody, most people might have said, "What a pity that a powerful preacher like Paul should have an audience of only one man a day, and a different one every day at that." But Paul could say, "God has enabled me to preach the Gospel to the whole Praetorian guard." And who knows how much the conversion of pagans in Rome may be attributed to Paul's being chained to the soldiers of the Praetorian guard?

When Paul wrote to the Corinthians, "I will come quickly to you, if the Lord wills," what he meant was that as soon as he learned what God's will was, he would do it quickly. We should allow no delay in carrying out God's will, once He has made it known to us. There are some Christians who have a sort of vague intention of doing God's will, but they think the doing of it can be postponed to a time in the far future. It's perfectly proper to wait until we clearly understand what God's will is, searching meanwhile to know that will and earnestly desiring to find it. But the moment that will is made plain to us, it's impossible to be too much in a hurry to fall into line with God's purpose.

The signs that God gives to indicate His will may differ in each of our lives. However, there are certain principles that should be followed carefully, to protect us from making mistakes. Here they are:

Consider the Word of God. God will never give us any light outside of that Word. If He says, "Repent," "Believe," "Be baptized," "Do not forsake the assembling of yourselves together," we need no further light on these matters.

Consider the promptings of conscience. If our conscience compels us to a certain course, and we have compared its promptings with the will of God as declared in the Scriptures, and they prove to be in agreement, there can be no doubt where our duty lies.

Consider the outward call. Is there a door opened before us for service? Is a path plainly set before us, and does God seem to point providentially to that path?

Consider the inward call. How do our hearts respond as we ponder what the will of God is? How do our hearts respond to the voices of the Word and of our conscience and to the outward call of God's providences?

If these four fail to make God's will clear, then we are to *use our rational judgment, our God-given intelligence.* God has given us our reasoning powers in order that we may determine questions of duty. Suppose you think God is calling you to a work for which you have no qualifications or strength. Then you may seriously question such an impression, for God would hardly call a blind man to be an artist, or a deaf man to sing in the choir, or a paralytic to be an itinerant evangelist.

And lastly, but most importantly, we must *use our spiritual judgment.* We should weigh the question before us in the scale of the whole soul. We should notice how in prayerful moments of intimate communion with God the question appears to us, and how it strikes us in carnal moments when we are tempted to be worldly-minded. We must trust the judgment of the soul when it is nearest to God.

What's Your Excuse, Christian?

Why was Paul so eager to go to Corinth quickly, if that should prove to be God's will? He gives the answer in the last part of I Corinthians 4:19, where he says, "And [I] will know, not the speech of them which are puffed up, but the power." He wanted to learn by personal observation what the real situation was among them.

In the phrase "And I shall know," the Greek word is *gnoosomai,* meaning knowledge gained from experience. Actually, the word "know" here is equivalent to "recognize" or "distinguish." In effect Paul was saying, "I am going to recognize what is what, and I'm not interested in the speech of those that are puffed up, but the power."

The word translated "speech" in Greek is *logon,* meaning also "logic, reason, expression." I believe what Paul was determined not to recognize among the Corinthians was their logical explanations for their non-Christian behavior. He knew they would be ready with intelligent and philosophical excuses for all their wrongdoing. "I am not going to accept them," he made clear to them even before he went among them. He then explains why he is going to reject such sophistries—because they are the words of those who are puffed up with a sense of their own importance. His feeling was that no matter how intelligent and logical the words of a proud person seem to be, they are not worth listening to.

In order to understand Paul's attitude, we must look back at verses 8 to 13 of this chapter. He said to the Corinthians, "Now ye are full, now ye are rich, ye have reigned as kings without us. . . ." And he contrasts his own life as an apostle, which was one of persecution and privation: "For I think that God hath set forth us the apostles last, as it were appointed to death: for we are made a spectacle unto the world, and to angels, and to men. We are fools for Christ's sake, but ye are wise in Christ; we are weak, but ye are strong; ye are honourable, but we are despised. Even unto this present hour we both hunger, and thirst, and are naked, and are buffeted, and have no certain dwellingplace; and labour, working with our own hands: being reviled, we bless; being persecuted, we suffer it: being defamed, we intreat: we are made as the filth of the world, and are the offscouring of all things unto this day."

How could the Corinthian Christians hope to outface him with excuses, after having read all this? Theirs was a life of ease and compromise; his was one of difficulties and faithfulness. "I know that you will try to excuse yourself," he is saying in effect. "You will speak arrogantly, out of your pride." To be selfish is bad enough. But to interpret selfish prosperity as the blessing of God, and to be proud of it, as the Corinthians did, was something Paul couldn't tolerate. "I won't swallow all that," is what Paul meant. The Corinthians were ready to tell Paul that they really had no opportunity to sacrifice; there was no need. I wonder what excuses our own generation of church people will render to God for living like kings and doing so little for others? I am not speaking of all, of course; but honestly, just how much are we willing to sacrifice for the cause of Christ?

I recently came across a poem called "Selfish Ambition" that expresses very clearly what I'm trying to get across:

I wanted to walk in the beaten path
  That was trod by the feet of men.
I wanted to thrive by the sweat of my brow,
  And rove in the valley of gain.
But the Master said,
  " 'Twas not thus I walked, nor lived;
  If so, I lived in vain."

I wanted to live with a selfish will;
  My logic was surely sane.
No thought had I for a hungry world
  Nor for those who suffered pain.
But the Master said,
  " 'Twas not thus I lived, nor gave;
  If so, I gave in vain."

I wanted to climb to a lofty height,
  To be known by the fame of men.
No care had I for the souls of men,
  Nor for death at the end of the lane.
But the Master said,
  " 'Twas not thus I lived, nor died;
  If so, I died in vain."

And so my all to Him I gave
  In consecration deep. For me
He loved and lived and gave and died.
  Then self died out of me.

—Zech Ford Bond

Profession Versus Possession

The Apostle Paul was a believer in that old saying, "What you are speaks so loudly I can't hear what you say." Although the saying was coined long after his day, he said practically the same thing to the Corinthian Christians in I Corinthians 4:19 when he told them he would recognize "not the speech of them which are puffed up, but the power.''

What is this power? The Greek word is *teen dunamin*. We could not say that it means ''miraculous manifestations,'' although the word *dunamis* in the New Testament occasionally means ''miracle indicative of the power energizing something not ordinarily and humanly possible.'' But here it stands in contrast to the words of the puffed up or proud. It means ''energy, deed, resultful activity.'' It can also mean the change in a person's life as a result of the operation of the grace of God. When a person receives Christ, he doesn't merely confess his faith with his mouth, but his whole life is transformed by the Holy Spirit.

As A. W. Tozer says: ''The truth received in power shifts the basis of life from Adam to Christ, and a new set of motives goes to work within the soul. A new and different Spirit enters the personality and makes the believing man new in every department of his being. His interests shift from things external to things internal, from things on earth to things in heaven. He loses faith in the soundness of external values; he sees clearly the deceptiveness of outward appearances; and his love for and confidence in the unseen and eternal world become stronger as his experience widens. . . . The gulf between theory and practice is so great as to be terrifying. . . . Wherever the Word comes without power its essential content is missed.

''Is justification from past offenses all that distinguishes a Christian from a sinner? Can a man become a believer in Christ and be no better than he was before? Does the Gospel offer no more than a skillful Advocate to get guilty sinners off free at the day of judgment? . . . The power of the Gospel changes him, shifts the basis of his life from self to

Christ, faces him about in a new direction, and makes him a new creation.

"The moral state of the penitent when he comes to Christ does not affect the result, for the work of Christ sweeps away both his good and his evil, and turns him into another man. The returning sinner is not saved by some judicial transaction apart from a corresponding moral change. Salvation must include a judicial change of status, but what is overlooked by most teachers is that it also includes an actual change in the life of the individual. And by this we mean more than a surface change; we mean a transformation as deep as the roots of his human life. If it does not go that deep, it does not go deep enough."

(See A. W. Tozer, *The Divine Conquered,* pp. 31-7.)

Paul was not going to be taken in by the words of the proud Corinthians but was going to look for evidences of the power of the Holy Spirit in their lives. And from the tenor of all that he wrote them, that power, which is the evidence of the effectiveness of the Gospel, was missing.

"Man is like an onion," said A. T. Pierson, "layer after layer, and each a layer of self in some form. Strip off self-righteousness and you will come to self-trust. Get beneath this and you will come to self-seeking and self-pleasing. Even when we think these are abandoned, self-will betrays its presence. When this is stripped off, we come to self-defense, just as the Corinthians did—the word of the puffed-up. And last of all, self-glory. When this seems to be abandoned, the heart of the human onion discloses pride that boasts of being truly humble."

Charles Kingsley said in his "Recipe for Misery: If you wish to be miserable, think about yourself; about what you want, what you like; what respect people ought to pay you; and then to you nothing will be pure. You will spoil everything you touch; you will make misery for yourself out of everything good; you will be as wretched as you choose.''

Can you suppose that the Corinthians were truly happy in their pride and bristling self-defensiveness? Paul's words must have stung deep and brought a feeling of shame that they tried to throw off by rationalizing their guilt and thinking up high-sounding philosophical phrases to justify their conduct.

Spurgeon writes: ''The shops in the square of San Marco were all religiously closed, for the day was a high festival. We were much disappointed, for it was our last day, and we desired to take away with us some souvenirs of lovely Venice; but our regret soon vanished, for on looking at the shop we meant to patronize we readily discovered signs of traffic within. We stepped to the side door and found, when one or two other customers had been served, that we might purchase to our heart's content, saint's day or no saint's day. After this fashion too many keep the laws of God to the eye but violate them in the heart. The shutters are up as if the man no more dealt with sin and Satan; but a brisk commerce is going on behind the scenes.''

How You Can Have Power

"For the kingdom of God is not in word, but in power" (I Cor. 4:20).

Restored in the Image of God

Why was the Apostle Paul so scornful of the "words" of the proud Corinthians? Was it not because he was looking for the practical effects of the Gospel upon the lives of the people? That's what he means by "power" in I Corinthians 4:20: "For the kingdom of God is not in word, but in power."

What does he mean by this statement? First of all, the Kingdom of God stands for the kingship, kingly rule, reign, the rulership of God in the life of man. It is expressed by the Greek word *basileia*, which refers to God's sovereignty or lordship over the world that He made, but particularly over humanity. The term "kingdom of heavens, or the heavens" means virtually the same thing. The latter term occurs mainly in Matthew's Gospel, which is

225

primarily addressed to the Jews. These people were so concerned lest they transgress the third commandment and take the name of God in vain when they spoke of the kingdom of God that they preferred to say "the kingdom of heaven, or the heavens." In Matthew 19:23, 24 the two terms are used interchangeably: "kingdom of heaven . . . kingdom of God."

When God created man He imparted to him His own image and likeness. That was a way of saying that our first parents, before they were driven out of the Garden of Eden, were like the God who made them, in that they possessed the power to lead a good life, as well as the gift of freedom to live by that power or to lose it by following the way of sin. Unfortunately they chose the way of disobedience, which was sin against God, and thus lost the power to do good. The fruit of the forbidden tree may have been sweet, as the pleasures of sin generally are, but after they had eaten came the knowledge that they were sinners. Thus began the pitiful story of rebellion against God, with all the misery and suffering that it entailed.

The Lord gave the Jewish nation the Law to deter them from evil. He allowed them to have human kings, such as David, who was the ideal king of Israel. Have you ever caught the full significance of Mark 2:23-28, which tells of the Lord and His disciples going through the cornfields on the Sabbath? Apparently they were hungry and began to pluck the grain. The Pharisees turned to Jesus and said, "Why do they on the sabbath day that which is not lawful?" Work was not permitted by Jewish law on the Sabbath, and plucking grain fell into this category.

The Lord's answer was most significant in revealing the superiority of David, King of Israel, over the Law. Referring to an event recorded in

I Samuel 21:1-6, He said: "Have ye never read what David did, when he had need, and was an hungred, he, and they that were with him? How he went into the house of God in the days of Abiathar the high priest, and did eat the shewbread, which is not lawful to eat but for the priests, and gave also to them which were with him?"

Why did the Lord bring this up? David as the ideal King of Israel was regarded as foreshadowing the Messianic King. This incident clearly showed that David as King could set himself above the Law. How much more, then, could Jesus, who came to be King of kings and Lord of lords? What the Law could not produce—the ideal life God intended for man when He first created him, to be free to choose evil and yet to choose only good—the Lord Jesus came to accomplish.

Consider also Mark 10:2-12, where the Lord is asked about divorce. He does not take sides with Moses in Deuteronomy 24:1, 3, but goes back to the account of creation and points out that God's original intention was the lifelong union of one man with one woman—an intention man failed to carry out. What the Lord is actually asserting is that He is going to restore God's original purpose for man in creation.

Power over sin was not possible after man's fall, even with the giving of the Law. Sad experience forces us to acknowledge that the enacting of rules or laws cannot make people righteous. The Law makes clear what constitutes sin or transgression, but it cannot produce the innate righteousness that makes it possible for people to carry out its commands. It may deter them through fear of punishment, but it has no power to change the nature of the individual. This is why laws, and police to enforce them, are not the real answer to crime. They can contain crime to some extent, but they are impotent to transform the criminal—sinner—transgressor—call him what you will.

Christ came to introduce the Kingdom of God, or the Gospel, which is not merely a deterrent power but a transforming and regenerating power. That's why Paul, in writing to the Corinthians, says, "For the kingdom of God is not in word, but in power."

An unknown poet has expressed it this way:

So let our lips and lives express
The holy Gospel we profess;
So let our words and virtues shine
To prove the doctrine all divine.

The Power to Live a Righteous Life

The Kingdom of God and the Gospel are synonymous. This is made clear in Mark 1:15, where John the Baptist is announcing the coming of Jesus' public ministry. "The time is fulfilled, and the kingdom of God is at hand," he says, and immediately adds, "repent ye, and believe the gospel." When is it possible for God really to reign in the human heart and life? Only when the sinner repents and allows Christ to give him new life—the birth from above of which He spoke to Nicodemus (John 3:1-15).

This is called the Gospel, or *euangelion*, "good news," because it tells us, not of man's involuntary subjugation by God, but of God's change produced in man so that the rulership or sovereignty—kingdom (*basileia*)—of God over him is not an occupation by a monarch but the loving, protective care of a Father. A Christian, that is, one who has been restored to God through the new birth, is not afraid or resentful of God's sovereignty but rejoices in it. This is why the Kingdom of God is not only

228

"power," but also, as Romans 14:17 says, "righteousness, and peace, and joy."

Thus power to live a righteous, peaceful, joyful life and to do good was not wholly restored to man till the coming of Jesus Christ. Great men and women, by their faith and prayers, did much to prepare the way for a new life of power over sin and evil; but not till the day of Christ and the new age He ushered in was that power fully restored. It came, like the strong arm of help, to assist fallen man in his effort to regain his foothold and become once more a child of God. The Apostle Paul expressed it in the familiar words of II Corinthians 5:19: "God was in Christ, reconciling the world unto himself, not imputing their trespasses unto them; and hath committed unto us the word of reconciliation."

The Gospel that Christ preached was the good news of the beginning, at least, of the re-establishment of God's original plan and purpose for man, that he should dominate over sin instead of being dominated by it. Christ justified us through His death; in other words, He took our place as the guilty sinner paying the penalty for sin, which is death. But Christ also changes us so completely that we become averse to sin. We no longer run after sin, although sin never ceases running after us.

Throughout the Old Testament, whatever earthly rulers were rightly or wrongly exercising sovereignty, we see that the real King of Israel (and of the world) is God. He may and does work through deputies, but no one can share His ultimate authority. Yet the frequent triumph of evil-doers and the misery of the righteous often made this fundamental Jewish conviction difficult to sustain. They felt that God must have put off some of His authority, and that He must one day assert His creative sovereignty again; and men longed for the coming of that "day"—a day which the prophet declared would surely come.

The fundamental message of Jesus' proclamation was that that day had now dawned. The things that many prophets and other righteous men had long desired to see and hear were now present before the eyes and in the ears of Jesus' disciples (Matt. 13:16ff., Luke 10:23f.). God's reign is here, or at least is so near at hand that already the signs of its activity are manifest; and men must make some response to the claims that it lays upon them.

The signs of God's rule were present in the work and words of Jesus Himself; they are proclaimed alike in His miracles and in His parables. They were not empty words but they were power. "For the kingdom of God is not in word, but in power." It's interesting to note that in the Greek text of this verse there is no verb. It does not read, "For the kingdom of God *is* not in word, but in power." It simply says, "For the kingdom of God not in word, but in power." There is no chronological limitation to this declaration. It was, is, and always shall be true. It is the permanent characteristic of the Kingdom of God.

It "is not in word." What does that mean? The Greek for "word" is *logoo,* which also means "logic and expression." It is not something pertaining to mere human intelligence and its expression through human utterance. Here *logoo,* "word," stands in contrast to *dunamei,* "power, energy." The reference is not to the fact that men should act rather than speak. It is to the fact that the work of man is valueless in comparison with the power of God.

Observe what Paul said previously, in verse 19—that he was not going to recognize the word of the proud. He was referring to the words of the Corinthians in regard to what they were or were not doing. They thought they were something special when actually they were falling far below God's norm for the Christian Church. Paul reminded them that what counted in their lives was the power of God—the power of the Kingdom of God. It is a contrast between the word and power of man—which are ineffective—and the Word of God which is the power of God unto salvation. Paul expressed it in Romans 1:16 when he said, "For I am not ashamed of the gospel of Christ [that's the Kingdom of God]: for it is the power of God unto salvation [that is, which results in salvation—the change and transformation of sinful man]."

The Word of the Proud

People who are proud of their abilities have a tendency to use them selfishly. They take credit to themselves for the gifts God has given them, and exploit them for their own benefit.

In I Corinthians 4, the Apostle Paul exposes the selfishness of the Corinthian Christians when he says, "Now ye are full, now ye are rich, ye have reigned as kings without us" (v. 8). That they had more than others is evident from the context. But instead of humbly rendering back to God what they were well able to give, they held on to it as though it was the result of their own unaided achievement. That's why Paul asked them the penetrating question in verse 7, "For who maketh thee to differ from another? and what hast thou that thou didst not receive? now if thou didst receive it, why dost thou glory, as if thou hadst not received it?"

Selfishness is the daughter of pride. But spiritual pride is a great hindrance to spiritual growth. Paul called the Corinthians "babes" because of their spiritual immaturity. "And I, breth-

231

ren, could not speak unto you as unto spiritual, but as unto carnal, even as unto babes in Christ" (I Cor. 3:1). They were gifted people, rich and eloquent, but there was something lacking in their characters.

A young preacher frequently talked with a wise old farmer. One day the question under discussion was, "What is the greatest hindrance to spiritual growth and happiness?" The preacher said, "Surely it is failure to renounce our sinful self." "No," said the farmer, "the greatest hindrance is failure to renounce our righteous self."

Man's desire is to blow himself up out of proportion. This sin is confined not merely to the unregenerate but is also one that often afflicts those who have experienced the new birth. The Corinthians to whom Paul wrote were believers. They had renounced their former sinful practices, but they had become puffed up with the notion that their righteousness was attributable to their own efforts. It was to the Laodicean church that the Lord said, "Thou sayest, I am rich, and increased with goods, and have need of nothing; and knowest not that thou art wretched, and miserable, and poor, and blind, and naked" (Rev. 3:17). Apparently the Corinthians talked a great deal about themselves in somewhat the same spirit as the Laodicean Christians, and that was something Paul couldn't stand. "I will come to you shortly, if the Lord will," he says in I Corinthians 4:19, "and will know, not the speech of them which are puffed up, but the power."

The proud are full of words. Actually in this verse the Greek text uses *ton logon,* "the word," for what is translated "the speech." Now notice Revelation 3:17, which I just quoted: "Because thou sayest, I am rich, etc." The verb in Greek here is

232

akin to *logos;* it is *legeis,* referring to an expression of the mind— *logos* (*legoo,* verb)—as contrasted with *lalia* (*laleoo,* verb), which is mere babbling not necessarily accompanied by thought. The Corinthians knew what they were saying. It was premeditated boasting. They prided themselves on their consecration yet gave little in comparison to what they kept for themselves. Like Peter they uttered words, but when it came to performance it was a different matter.

> Beware of Peter's boastful words,
> Nor confidently say,
> "I never will deny Thee, Lord,"
> But "Grant I never may."

There are many people who would not kill a mouse without publicizing it, but Samson killed a lion and said nothing about it. Say much of what the Lord has done for you. Say little of what you have done for the Lord.

Remember the account of Ananias and Sapphira in Acts 5? They had a parcel of land that they were going to sell, and they said they would give all the proceeds to the Lord. But when it came to actual performance they gave only part, declaring it to be the whole. They were show-offs who were punished for their sin of lying to the Lord. They had spoken words in pride. Isn't it comforting that the Lord doesn't strike those of us dead today who are full of proud utterances, but whose acts are not commensurate with our words? If God acted uniformly in such matters, there would be few of us around, I'm afraid.

Apparently the Corinthian Christians were saying to Paul, "Come over and you'll hear of what we are doing." Paul responded, "I'll come to you

233

quickly, if God wills, but I'm not going to recognize 'the word' of you who are puffed up." He could have known the power of their lives at a distance.

It reminds me of Aesop's fable about the traveler who was entertaining some men in a tavern with an account of the wonders he had done abroad. "I was once at Rhodes," said he, "and the people of Rhodes, you know, are famous for jumping. Well, I took a jump there that no other man could come within a yard of. That's a fact; and if we were there I could bring you ten men who would prove it." "What need is there to go to Rhodes for witnesses?" asked one of his hearers. "Just imagine you are there now and show us your leap."

Thus Paul intimated to the Corinthians, "I don't have to come to listen to your words. You can prove the quality of your life by what you do, and I'll know it from where I am."

Thy Kingdom Come

Some people have been perplexed by the Lord's statement in Mark 9:1, "Verily I say unto you, That there be some of them that stand here, which shall not taste of death, till they have seen the kingdom of God come with power." (See also Matt. 16:28, Luke 9:27.) This does not refer to the future Kingdom—the culmination of what has begun with the first coming of the Lord—but to the coming of the Kingdom as the power of Christ to save man. What our Lord was saying was that these people would see His power manifested through His crucifixion and resurrection. These words were part and parcel of Christ's prophecy concerning His forthcoming passion and triumph. That was the demonstration of the power of God's Kingship.

The Kingdom of God is the dominant theme of the recorded teachings of the Lord Jesus. It is most strikingly presented in His parables. Some of these are described as parables of the Kingdom. For example, in the Parable of the Seed Growing Secretly recorded in Mark 4:26-29, the stress is on the fact that the germination and growth of a seed is a process with which man has nothing to do.

The following parable, that of the Mustard Seed (vv. 30-32), contrasts the proverbially tiny mustard seed with the large plant that grows from it. The Kingdom of God resembles these processes; there is the power of God behind them, like the elemental power that forces a blade of grass through the earth. The ministry of the Lord Jesus corresponds to sowing time rather than to harvest; at present the Kingdom of God is germinal rather than complete. Its consummation is as sure as the harvest, but that time is not yet. (See also the Parable of the Sower, Mark 4:3ff.)

The presence of this germinal Kingdom of God challenges the men among whom it stands, and calls for a decision while there is yet time, before the final harvest makes it too late. The members of the Kingdom of God are not the so-called righteous (Mark 2:17), the proud and self-satisfied Pharisees, but repentant sinners. (See the Parable of the Great Supper, Luke 14:16-24; the Parable of the Pharisee and the Publican, Luke 18:9-14; and the Parable of the Two Sons, Matt. 21:28-31.)

Thus, the Kingdom of God, as it is presented in the teaching and work of Jesus, is essentially God's Kingdom and not ours. It is something that proceeds from God, not something men build. It is not a utopia or a new social order, and it is not a mere disposition within men's hearts. It is an act of God Himself; it is His initiative in breaking the power of evil.

But, just because in the ministry of Jesus the

Kingdom was present in germinal rather than finished form, men still have their part to play: they must make a response to God's offer of His Kingdom. The Kingdom of God has come so near as to provoke an unavoidable crisis. It is now up to men to draw near to the Kingdom of God, and their response to it is shown by their attitude to the Lord Jesus Christ Himself. For it is in the person and deeds of Christ that God's reign has actively begun, that the assault against evil, physical and spiritual, has been launched. Men's acceptance or rejection of God's Kingdom is thus inevitably expressed by their attitude to the Lord Jesus. This truth was clearly seen by the Pharisees and by Caiaphas; no mere technical dispute or personal quarrel gave rise to their determination to destroy Him. Jesus Christ had come to do what their Law could never accomplish—to restore God's damaged and perverted creation to its original destiny in perfect obedience to His will.

Although the Kingdom of God as power to save began with the Lord Jesus, that does not mean that God's plan of fully restoring the world to its original state is not still to come. Christ is going to finish the work He started. God's reign is still to be established; and it is in this sense that Jesus bids His disciples pray, "Thy kingdom come." In the absolute sense, God's Kingdom will not come until the return of the Lord in absolute power, no longer to save but to bring punishment and retribution.

It is generally in this latter sense that the expression, "Kingdom of God," is used in the New Testament, outside the Gospels, as denoting that Kingdom which is the reward and goal in heaven of the Christian life here below. The Kingdom of God began with the Lord Jesus as the power to save individuals, and it will come fully as the Lord returns in power to restore His whole creation to Himself.

> Jesus is coming to earth again—
> What if it were today?
> Coming in power and love to reign—
> What if it were today?
> Coming to claim His chosen Bride,
> All the redeemed and purified,
> Over this whole earth scattered wide—
> What if it were today?
>
> Faithful and true would He find us here,
> If He should come today?
> Watching in gladness and not in fear,
> If He should come today?
> Signs of His coming multiply;
> Morning light breaks in eastern sky;
> Watch, for the time is drawing nigh—
> What if it were today?

Power to Overcome Fear

The Greek word for "power" in I Corinthians 4:20 is *dunamis*. Some years ago, when an inventor developed a highly explosive substance, he used this Greek word to coin a name for it: dynamite. That's what "power" is, in the New Testament meaning of the word. As Christians, we have received this great power to live a victorious life against sin. It's not our own power but the power of God within us. It's power to live above circumstances instead of allowing them to toss us about like a football. It's power to live as poor men for Christ's sake when we might have had the opportunity and ability to be rich.

When Paul made his intended visit to the Corinthians, he didn't want to listen to their proud words but "to know the power," he said in verse 19.

"For the kingdom of God is not in word, but in power" (v. 20). In other words, if God is King of your life, that will not result in boastfulness but in performance.

When Paul speaks of the transforming power of God, he calls it "the power," to distinguish it from all other kinds of influence. It was the power he himself had experienced as he traveled on the road to Damascus. It was an overcoming force that neutralized his pharisaism and resistance to Christ. This power of Christ manifested itself in the transformation of proud Saul, who was persecuting the Christians, to Paul, the humble and persecuted believer who was ready to suffer anything for the sake of Christ whom he had previously despised. And this power manifested itself in his ministry of preaching the Gospel as "the power of God unto salvation to every one that believeth" (Rom. 1:16).

Paul realized that this power was not only "unto salvation" but was God's endowment to the believer to enable him to overcome sin and live a Christlike life. What amazing changes it wrought in his life, and it can do the same in ours. Consider that Hindu woman who was converted by hearing the Word of God. She was terribly persecuted by her husband, and a missionary asked her, "How do you react to his cruel treatment?" Smiling, she replied, "Sahib, I try to cook better food for him. When he speaks unkindly to me, I answer softly. I want to show him that when I became a Christian I became a better wife and mother." In time a change took place in her husband. He had been able to withstand the preaching of the missionary, but he could not withstand the practicing of his Christlike wife. She had the joy of winning him to Christ.

When the apostles received the power of the Holy Spirit, what difference did it make in their lives? What kind of enablement does the power of God bring to men? It enables them to quit certain sins and wrong practices and acquire virtues and practices that are characteristics of a transformed life.

What a man loses by receiving such power can be summed up in one word: fear. He is no longer afraid of doing what is right in the sight of God, even though he knows it may cost him something. Paul expressed the difference that God makes in a person's life in II Timothy 1:7, "For God hath not given us the spirit of fear; but of power, and of love, and of a sound mind." Where the power of God is, fear is absent. There was real danger that Timothy would suffer persecution in Ephesus as a result of his Christian testimony, and be tempted to deny the faith. He was known as Paul's friend, and Paul was in jail for Christ's sake. That's why Paul wrote to Timothy, "Be not thou therefore ashamed of the testimony of our Lord, nor of me his prisoner: but be thou partaker of the afflictions of the gospel according to the power of God" (II Tim. 1:8).

When this power comes upon you, fear of witnessing disappears, and a desire to sacrifice and suffer for Christ's sake emerges. Unfortunately, that was not what happened to the Corinthian Christians. They neither sacrificed nor suffered for Christ. They were fearful that to do so would result in their being in want. But as for Paul and Timothy, their testimony was "For God hath not given us the spirit of fear; but of power, and of love, and of a sound mind."

The Greek word translated "fear" in this verse is *deilias* (*deilia,* nominative), which is better rendered as "cowardice." When the power of Christ comes upon us through His Holy Spirit, we cease to be cowards. God supplies us with the courage to stand up to the world and to Satan instead of compromising. Cowardice always weakens the Christian. Fearfulness leads to impotence. The man who distrusts himself is paralyzed by his distrust and accomplishes nothing. Why did the man who received one talent bury it? "I was afraid," he said (Matt. 25:25). Cowardice is disabling. All the strength of a fearful man is drained away by his own hesitancies and timidities.

John Newton wrestled with this problem and came up with the following declaration of faith:

Why should I fear the darkest hour,
Or tremble at the tempter's power?
Jesus vouchsafes to be my tower.

Against me earth and hell combine,
But on my side is power divine:
Jesus is all, and He is mine.

Power That Changes Lives

The characteristic of the Spirit-filled Christian is power. Christians should be dynamos. Christ promised His disciples, "Ye shall receive power, after that the Holy Ghost is come upon you" (Acts 1:8). That's what happened at Pentecost. The 12 disciples had kept themselves locked in the upper room for fear of what the enemies of the Gospel would do to them. When the Holy Spirit came upon them, they lost that fear. They flung the doors open and went forth to preach the Gospel.

The Apostle Paul felt that the Corinthian Christians should have lost their fear of privation, defamation, and persecution. But they preferred ease to sacrifice. Isn't that true of most Christians today? They give so little room to God's Holy Spirit. They do so little and yet become so proud and puffed up. If Paul were to look down upon us today,

240

he'd say, "I don't want to hear the words of the puffed up ones but to know the power."

The Holy Spirit is the One who makes the difference between an ineffectual life and a power-filled one. Take Peter as an example. He was a miserable coward at one time. With the rest of the disciples he forsook Christ and fled from the garden. Three times he denied that he knew Christ. He was afraid of having to suffer for Him. But what a difference Pentecost made! He stood up before vast crowds and fearlessly proclaimed the Gospel. In Acts 4:13 we read, "Now when they saw the boldness of Peter and John, and perceived that they were unlearned and ignorant men, they marvelled."

When you have this power, you acquire an intuitive knowledge of the unknown and the unseen. The difference between the Corinthians and Paul was a matter of values. The Corinthians thought chiefly of the comfort of material things, while Paul was willing to forego these when necessary because he thought of himself primarily as a citizen of heaven. He didn't care as much about the applause of men as he did about the approval of angels, and most of all God. "For we are made a spectacle unto the world, and to angels, and to men" (I Cor. 4:9). In other words, when men make fun of your self-sacrificing dedication to Christ, angels praise you. The cowardly Christian can hear only the ridicule of men. He knows nothing of the praise of angels.

The power of the Holy Spirit gives knowledge of the unseen spiritual realities that the coward has no eyes to see. The fearful believer (what a contradiction of terms!) sees only the cross, while the courageous Spirit-filled Christian can see the resurrection. Power makes soldiers brave and enables them to envision the victory beyond the battle. If you cannot see God in the difficulties of life, you lack the power of which Paul spoke.

John Henry Jowett has beautifully expressed what characterizes this life of power. "Another element in a forceful character is heat, the fire of an unquenchable enthusiasm. . . . The Acts of the Apostles is a burning book. There is no cold or lukewarm patch from end to end. The disciples had been baptized with fire, with the holy, glowing enthusiasm caught from the altar of God.

"They had this central fire, from which every other purpose and faculty in the life gets its strength. This fire in the apostles' soul was like a furnace-fire in a great liner, which drives her through the tempests and through the envious and engulfing deep. Nothing could stop these men. Nothing could hinder their going. 'We cannot but speak the things that we have seen and heard.' 'We must obey God rather than men.' This strong imperative rings throughout all their doings and all their speech. They have heat, and they have light, because they were baptized by the power of the Holy Ghost."

(John Henry Jowett, *Things That Matter Most*, p. 251. Also see J. D. Jones, *The Unfettered Word*, pp. 123-130.)

Paul told the Corinthians that when he came to them he would know the power. How can you know power? By experiencing its force. When you are empty this power fills you. When you are weak it strengthens you. When you are pushed and restrained you know it. When the disciples received the Holy Spirit at Pentecost, there was activity, there was noise, there were tongues of fire, there was speech, there were people repenting of their sins as a result of each one hearing the Gospel in his own tongue. When you have this power it not only affects your own life but the lives of others.

The life of Paul was one that demonstrated the power of God. His ministry was unique. We read of no one else doing what he did, going from nation to nation, entering a city without knowing a single face, leaving it containing hundreds of men and women who would thank God throughout eternity that they had ever seen him. He entered Corinth a stranger and left it having brought into being a church of believers, despite the fact that it was one of the most sinful cities in the world. After visiting Thessalonica for only three weeks, he wrote: "Our gospel did not come to you in word only, but also in power. . . . and ye became imitators of us and of the Lord. . . . Ye turned to God, to serve a living and true God, and to wait for his Son from heaven" (I Thess. 1:5,6, 9, 10).

Apply the Proper
Discipline When Needed

"What will ye? shall I come unto you with a rod, or in love, and in the spirit of meekness?" (I Cor. 4:21).

Accepting Rebuke in the Right Spirit

When you see something wrong going on in a Christian church, what ought you to do about it? Is it the Christian's responsibility to rebuke a fellow believer?

In the 4th chapter of I Corinthians, Paul spoke out strongly against the attitude of the Corinthian Christians, contrasting their selfish and proud affluence with the apostolic example of personal sacrifice for the sake of the Gospel. "You have enriched yourselves," he says in verse 8, "while we go hungry and thirsty." He wanted to counsel them in a way that would cause them properly to evaluate the priorities of the Christian life.

One of the most difficult decisions we have to make is what to put first, second, third, or last in our lives. Paul was determined to put Christ first. The

Corinthians apparently had not done this. This troubled Paul, since he had adopted them as his spiritual children (see v. 15).

What really upset Paul about the behavior of the Corinthians was that they seemed proud of their selfish attitudes. It's bad enough to be selfish, but to be proud of it compounds the guilt. Paul attributed the worsening of such attitudes to the fact that he was not personally in Corinth to teach them. Lack of adequate teaching was apparently greatly to blame. That's why he decided to send Timothy to Corinth. He wanted to go himself and told them he would do so shortly, if the Lord willed.

The Kingdom of God had become empty theory to the Corinthians instead of a demonstration of the power of the Holy Spirit. As a spiritual father, Paul sternly warned them that when he came he would rebuke them and set things right among them. At the beginning of this chapter, Paul had defended himself against the criticism of the Corinthians. Now he goes on to exercise his apostolic authority of discipline. The Corinthians did not want to accept his discipline, denying him the right to exercise the authority of an apostle since he was not one of the original twelve disciples chosen by Christ.

In I Corinthians 9 Paul defends his apostleship by saying, "Am I not an apostle? am I not free? have I not seen Jesus Christ our Lord? are not ye my work in the Lord? If I be not an apostle unto others, yet doubtless I am to you: for the seal of mine apostleship are ye in the Lord" (vv. 1, 2).

In I Corinthians 4:21, therefore, Paul is not acting as an individual believer rebuking fellow believers but in his divinely appointed office as an apostle. He is acting as the Corinthians' spiritual father. He is not even seeking the corporate action of the church, as he does in the next chapter. In a family, the father exercises his disciplinary privilege without seeking the agreement of the rest of the family.

Paul indicates that the correction he desired to bring about could be accomplished in either of two ways: through punishment, by using the "rod," just as a father does when spanking his son; or through the persuasive power of words. Do you want me to come and spank you, or to counsel you in love? is his thought here. The choice, apparently, would be determined by their attitude. This indicates that both ways are permissible to the leader of the flock, depending on which will be more fruitful. In Paul's case, the attitude of the Corinthians would determine which method he would use. Isn't that comparable to how we parents act? Sometimes we find it necessary to spank, and at other times a word of reproof proves sufficient.

That the Corinthians needed correction, Paul had not the slightest doubt. Of course, they would deny this. But as an apostle he had made the diagnosis and was determined to apply the remedy. How foolishly we sometimes act in the spiritual realm. When a doctor tells us there is something wrong with our physical bodies, we recognize his expertise and accept the treatment he prescribes. We don't react with piqued pride when he tells us how we can have a blemish removed from our bodies. We willingly pay the price the physician asks to free us from a wart or other mark of disfigurement. Why, then, should we turn away with wounded pride from any mirror that presumes to throw back to us a reflection of our moral blemishes?

When it comes to our spiritual health, we want to make our own diagnosis and apply our own rules. We act like petulant babies, thrusting away the medicine that would make us well, because we find it unpalatable. We become angry with the wise spiritual leader and counselor who presumes to point out how we are harming ourselves and others by our unchristian behavior. We're like the King of Israel who said of Micaiah the prophet, "But I hate him; for he doth not prophesy good concerning me, but evil" (I Kings 22:8).

Nevertheless, the King was persuaded to call for Micaiah; and the friendly servant who went to call him warned him to speak "that which is good," lest he incur the King's wrath. But Micaiah replied in the spirit of a true prophet of God, "As the Lord liveth, what the Lord saith unto me, that will I speak" (I Kings 22:14). That was the spirit of the apostle Paul in exercising his authority in the church, as conferred upon him by Christ.

Lack of Discipline Means Lack of Love

When you love someone very much, it's hard to have to rebuke that person for a fault that is harming him and others. In the first place, you may be afraid he'll reject your words and love you the less. Something like that must have been going through the Apostle Paul's mind as he felt it necessary to correct the faults that were harming the testimony of the Corinthian church.

Paul didn't want to estrange himself from the Corinthians and cause them to hate him. He knew the words of wisdom found in Proverbs 9:7-9: "He that reproveth a scorner getteth to himself shame: and he that rebuketh a wicked man getteth himself a blot. Reprove not a scorner, lest he hate thee: rebuke a wise man, and he will love thee. Give instruction to a wise man, and he will be yet wiser: teach a just man, and he will increase in learning." In the light of those words, Paul wanted to make sure of the best way to administer necessary reproof.

Reproof is sometimes unskillfully administered and at other times unfaithfully withheld. Paul did not want to pursue either course. He wanted skillfully to administer needed rebuke.

Another admonition with which Paul was familiar is found in Proverbs 13:24: "He that spareth his rod hateth his son." If the rod is necessary, one should not hesitate to administer it. Paul loved the Corinthians as his own spiritual children. He would have been more popular among them had he been indifferent to their wrong ways. But he wouldn't have been faithful in the execution of his fatherly love. The father who avoids the application of the rod because it's easier not to incur the possible resentment of his son is actually a selfish father. Parents who are in the habit of giving their children everything they ask, and of permitting them to disobey without punishment, really do not love their children as much as they think they do. "He that spareth his rod hateth his son." To call it love is to be deceived by one of Satan's lies. The man who gravely tells his child what is wrong, and, if the wrong is repeated, strictly chastens him—that man really loves his child, and sacrifices his own ease for the child's highest good.

Paul considered the Corinthian Christians rough diamonds in need of grinding and polishing. The Koh-I-Noor diamond, when it came into the Queen of England's possession, was a misshapen lump. It was necessary to have its corners cut off and its sides reduced to symmetry. But no unskillful hand was permitted to touch it. Men of science were summoned to consider its nature and capacities. They examined the form of its crystals and the consistency of its parts. They considered the direction of the grain and the side on which it would bear pressure. With their instructions, the jewel was placed in the hands of an experienced lapidary, and by long, patient, careful labor its sides were ground down to the desired proportions. The gem was hard and needed a heavy pressure. It was precious and needed every precaution that science and skill could suggest to get it polished into shape without cracking it in the process. The effort was successful. The hard diamond was rubbed down into forms of beauty and yet sustained no damage by the greatness of the pressure to which it was subjected.

"Jewels, bright jewels," in the form of spiritual children were the heritage God gave to Paul as a spiritual father. God may permit us to play the same role as spiritual parents to our children, or to the children of God in the Church, in the case of pastors and teachers. Let us recognize in either case that children are unshapely and need to be polished; they are hard, and cannot be reduced to symmetry without firm handling; they are brittle, and so liable to be permanently damaged by the wrong kind of pressure; but they are stones of peculiar preciousness and, if they are successfully polished, they will shine as stars for ever and ever, giving off the glory they reflect from the Sun of righteousness. Those in whose care and trust God has placed these diamonds in the rough should neither strike them unskillfully nor let them lie uncut and unpolished.

While there should be a strong manly love to wield the rod firmly, there should also be a farseeing wisdom to judge in view of all the circumstances, whether and when the rod should be applied. A parent must study carefully both his child's character and his own.

There's no inherent virtue in bodily pain to heal a moral or spiritual ailment. Much depends on the adaptation of punishment in kind and measure to the particular form of the child's misbehavior. If a child is seldom or never so wayward as to need the rod, then seldom or never let the rod be applied. But be careful not to determine or proclaim beforehand that you will never resort to corporal punishment, lest you be setting your wisdom against the law of the Lord.

The rod and love are not antagonistic. It's not necessary to banish one in order to live under the rule of the other. Love keeps the rod, and lays it on when needful. Our Father in heaven chastens every child whom He loves, and does not spare for their crying. Genuine parental love on earth follows the divine example.

(See William Arnot, *Laws from Heaven for Life on Earth,* pp. 359-66.)

Less Talk and More Walk

A Quaker had a bundle of hides stolen from his warehouse. He began to wonder what steps he should take to prevent a repetition of such an act. Instead of putting the machinery of the law in motion, he inserted the following ad in the newspapers: "Whoever stole a quantity of hides on the 5th of this month is hereby informed that the owner has a sincere wish to be his friend. If poverty tempted him to take this false step, the owner will keep the whole transaction secret, and will gladly put him in the way of obtaining money by means more likely to bring him peace of mind."

A few nights later, when the family were about to retire to rest, a man knocked at the door of the Quaker's house, and he carried with him a bundle of skins. "I have brought them back," he said. "It is the first time I ever stole anything, and I have felt very bad about it." "Let it be the last, friend," said the Quaker. "The secret still lies between ourselves." He spoke to the man faithfully and affectionately about the folly of dishonesty, and of the claims of the Gospel. He also took him into his employ and the man became a changed character, living an exemplary life from then on.

Paul was hoping something like that would happen in the case of the proud Corinthians—that his single word of admonition would really suffice. He had no desire to go to them in a punitive spirit, but in a spirit of love and kindly counsel. Where "a word to the wise is sufficient," there is no need of stronger measures. Wielding the rod should be the last resort, only after verbal persuasion has failed to bring about the desired results.

Later on, in II Corinthians, we see that Paul's hopes were realized. His words stung the Corinthians to a zealous purging of the sin in their midst, so that they almost went to the other extreme of being too harsh with the sinning members. Paul had to admonish them about this, also, and urge them to comfort the repentant and downcast sinner, lest he be "swallowed up with overmuch sorrow" (II Cor. 2:7).

His purpose in all this was that the "power" of God might be manifested in the Corinthian church, rather than the bombast of "great swelling words." Surely this is what is needed in the Church today: less talk and more walk. Would you like to see results in your service for Christ? Whether you're a pastor, a Sunday school teacher, or simply a lay person in the home or the business world, you need the power of God to make your witness effective. This power must first of all be manifested *in* you before it can flow out *from* you.

How do you secure this power within? There's no mystery about it; God's Word makes it very simple. You believe in Christ as the Son of God and receive Him into your heart by faith. That results in your salvation from sin and deliverance from eternal condemnation. But to have His power, you must be "attached" to Him as a branch is attached to a vine. The branch has no life or fruitbearing power apart from the vine, and you can have none apart from a constant abiding in Christ—relinquishing your so-called right to self-determination in complete submission to His will and plan for your life.

That's what the Apostle Paul did, and his name rings down the corridors of time as the most fruitful and power-filled witness of the early Church.

The Christian who wants to be greatly used of God must first count the cost and decide whether he is willing to pay it. As Jesus Himself said: "Whosoever doth not bear his cross, and come after me, cannot be my disciple. For which of you, intending to build a tower, sitteth not down first, and counteth the cost, whether he have sufficient to finish it? Lest haply, after he hath laid the foundation, and is not able to finish it, all that behold it begin to mock him, Saying, This man began to build, and was not able to finish" (Luke 14:27-30).

Paul accepted that challenge, saying in Philippians 3:7, 8, "What things were gain to me, those I counted loss for Christ. Yea doubtless, and I count all things but loss for the excellency of the knowledge of Christ Jesus my Lord."

Here is a prayer of dedication by an unknown author that the Apostle Paul himself could heartily make his own. Can you?

"O Lord, I present myself to Thee: my will, my time, my talents, my tongue, my property, my reputation, my entire being, to be—and to do—anything Thou requirest of me. Now, as I have given myself to Thee, I am no longer my own, but all the Lord's. I believe that Thou wilt accept the offering I bring. I trust Thee to work in me all the good pleasure of Thy will. I am willing to receive what Thou givest, to lack what Thou withholdest, to relinquish what Thou takest, to surrender what Thou claimest, to suffer what Thou ordainest, to do what Thou commandest, to wait—till Thou sayest, 'Go.' "

I

INDEX OF SUBJECTS

II

INDEX OF ILLUSTRATIONS

III

INDEX OF ENGLISH WORDS

IV

INDEX OF GREEK WORDS

gumniteuoo	be dressed in		
	rags	4:11	115
gumnos	naked	4:11	115
heis, (hen)	one	John 10:30	145
heteros	another	4:6	31
	(of a different kind)		
heuriskoo	find	Phil. 2:6-8	16
(*heuretheis*)			
hina	so that	4:6	24, 40
hoos	as if	4:9	75, 76
hos [hoi] [ha]	who, which, what	4:6	26
houtos	this	4:6	26
(*tauta*)			
hupomonee	patience with things	Rom. 15:5	137
ischuros	strong	4:10	96
kale-oo	call	4:13	146
katharma	scouring	4:13	153
kolaphizoo	strike	4:11	116
		Matt. 26:67	
kopia-oo	labor	4:12	122
korennumi	fill	4:8	64
(*kekoresmenoi*)	(with food)	Acts 27:38	
(*koresthentes*)			
kosmos	world	4:9, 13	86, 152
lale-oo	speak	4:19	233
lalia	speech	4:19	233
lambanoo	take	Phil. 2:6-8	14
(*laboon*)			
legoo	speak, say	4:12, 19	232, 233
		I Pet. 3:9	131
logos	word	4:19, 20	218, 230
loidore-oo	insult	4:12, 13	127, 128
[loidoroumenoi]		John 9:28	130, 142
[loidorein]		Acts 23:4	
[eloidoreesan]		I Pet. 2:23	
loidoria	calumny	I Tim. 5:14	130
		I Pet. 3:9	
loidoros	reviler	5:11	128
		6:10	
		I Tim. 5:14	
		I Pet. 3:9	

makarios	blessed	Matt. 5:1-10	92, 131
		Luke 6:20-24	
makariotees	blessedness	Matt. 5:1-10	92
		Luke 6:20-24	
makarizoo	bless	Luke 1:48	131, 132
		James 5:11	
makrothumia	patience	4:12	137
	with persons	Rom. 2:4	
makrothumos	longsuffering	4:12	137
manthanoo	learn	4:6	26
meta	after	4:6	12
metamorpho-omai	transfigure	4:6	13, 16
metascheematizoo	assume a figure,	4:6	12, 13, 16
	refashion	II Cor. 11:14	17, 24
		Phil. 3:21	
mimeetees	imitator	4:16	182
morphee	form	Phil. 2:6-8	14, 15, 18
nous	mind	4:14	162
nouthesia	warning	4:14	163
nouthete-oo	admonish	4:14	162, 163
oneidizoo	revile	4:13	130, 142
		Matt. 5:11	
ophelon	would that	4:8	66
oude	not	4:13	153
ousia	substance	Phil. 2:6-8	14
paida goo gos	instructor	4:15	168
pais	child	4:15	168
para	near	4:13	146
paradidoomi	deliver	15:3	32
(*paredooka*)			
paradosis	tradition	11:2	32, 33
		II Thess. 2:15	
parakleetos	beseecher	4:16	180
parakale-oo	entreat	4:13, 16	146, 147
(*parakleetheesowtai*)			
Matt. 5:4			
			179, 180
(*parakaloumen*)		Matt. 26:53	
pas	all, every	4:13	152

Other Books on I Corinthians
by Spiros Zodhiates

A Richer Life
I Corinthians 1; 487 pages.

A Revolutionary Mystery
I Corinthians 2; 278 pages.

Getting the Most Out of Life
I Corinthians 3; 380 pages.

You and Public Opinion
I Corinthians 4:1-5; 200 pages.

Tongues?
I Corinthians 12—14; 192 pages.

To Love is to Live
I Corinthians 13; 365 pages.

Conquering the Fear of Death
I Corinthians 15; 869 pages.